THE SCREENWRITER'S WAY

BRIAN CRAFT

THE SCREENWRITER'S WAY: SECOND EDITION MASTER COURSE

ISBN: 9798359487153

CONTENTS

Dedicated to:

All those with the courage to tell their story.

PREFACE

STORYTELLING has proven itself an endless and wonderful adventure for me. My desire to write began, much like I imagine it has for you, as an indefinable urge to create the kinds of stories and books and movies that first inspired me. That inspiration turned into an adventure that has transformed me. It took me to many parts of the world where I met amazing people and had fantastic experiences. It helped me learn who I was and how to express myself. Eventually my storytelling met my life-story and they became eternally intertwined. Of course, they always had been, but by the time I'd taken my own Hero's Journey, I understood why.

Part of my journey included an intense mastery of creative process, developed while working as an international product designer. As I turned my creative life toward storytelling, I took that knowledge of process and filled it with hundreds of books on storytelling, writing, screenwriting, and filmmaking. Then went on to study screenwriting at UCLA's School of Theater, Film, and Television and transformed all that I learned into a writer's process that helped me create some award-caliber screenplays.

Soon, other writer's began asking me for my writer's process and tools. That inspired the first edition of **The Screenwriter's Way.**

Since writing and publishing it in 2013, it has sold all around the world and helped a lot of new and seasoned writers advance their knowledge of storytelling and screenwriting. It helped create screenplays that won or placed in competitions, found options or sold, landed writers assignments, and some were even produced.

What I didn't anticipate was that the book would create a platform for writer's to approach me with so many questions. They not only asked about concepts in the book, but also issues beyond the scope of the first edition like living the writer's life and finding ideas. It spawned a lot of great interactions and elevated my own adventure as a writer, and then as educator, and even as mentor.

Now, farther down the road, and I hope a little wiser, I wanted to clarify and further develop the original book's concepts as part of my own journey and process, and so, decided to expand upon the first edition. In doing so, I decided to answer many of those burning writer questions I'd been asked so often along the way.

To that end, all of the chapters from the First Edition were revisited and received great additions to clarify and advance the concepts for this new Second Edition. There are also several insightful new chapters that address developing ideas through your intuition, doing creative research, and identifying the personal convictions in your writing.

Storytelling is a lifelong adventure. You'll never stop learning how to do it, and the more you learn, the more it grows to teach you. I believe that adopting an open-minded philosophy of growth and exploration immediately eases the pressure on any creative mind. You aren't perfect. Your writing won't be perfect. You won't nail storytelling in the first attempt, and maybe not the one-hundredth. But with the tools in the coming pages you'll learn to communicate your ideas clearer and with greater truth. Along the way to your own writing transformation, you'll inspire some people with your work, and I dare say, you can change the world with a good story.

So if you got this far, you've already stepped into your adventure. I'm with you. The knowledge of my mentors is with you. And the Screenwriter's Way is your guide for at least part of your journey.

To quote the legendary mythologist and author Joseph Campbell:

"For we have not even to risk the adventure alone, for the heroes of all time have gone before us."

I firmly believe that by the time you finish the process in this book you'll be a better writer. But most importantly, I believe The Screenwriter's Way introduces you to a way of systematically developing your personal story, your own hero's journey.

If you choose to dedicate yourself to storytelling and developing your process, your storytelling and your life story will eventually converge into something powerful like mine did.

You will become the hero of your own adventure.

"THE CALL TO ADVENTURE SIGNIFIES THAT **DESTINY HAS SUMMONED THE HERO.**"

- JOSEPH CAMPBELL

THE HERO WITH A THOUSAND FACES

(THAT HERO IS YOU.)

INTRODUCTION

THE SCREENWRITER'S WAY >>>>>

Something about stories drives the human mind. We have the ability to be taken away by them and transported to someplace else, defying time and space and even reality. We live inside the characters we find in those places. We make friends with them and feel their happiness and pain and triumphs and failures. The really amazing part is that by experiencing their journeys we actually learn about our own lives. Sometimes you only learn a little, other times you take away something so profound that it might change the entire direction of your life.

Movies are unique in the world of storytelling. Science tells us that our brains can't distinguish a movie from a dream, or a dream from real life. So when you see a movie you experience it more intensely than any other story form.

That happened to me for the first time when I was a kid and I experienced Star Wars on the big screen. It was a cannon shot into my world and ignited a great passion for stories and especially for movies that has been lifelong.

In time, I became compelled to tell my own stories to the world. I felt had something to say. I had some emotional spark inside me that I wanted someone else to experience too. **That's what we do as artists; we use our craft to convey our emotions to another person in hopes of getting them to feel the emotion that we did.** That act joins us together. It gives us a shared understanding of the world. And our journeys, at least in part, become one.

But my first screenplays were rough to say the least. However, I knew a lot about building a creative process from being trained as a product designer before I was a screenwriter. I knew that there had to be a process for writing and that it would help me bring my ideas to life. I also realized that the roadblock to getting a nebulous idea from my head to the screen was the craft that embodies screenwriting itself. **That means the craft of story design is both the path, and the obstacle you must first overcome.**

The Screenwriter's Way is a creative writer's process, designed to be simple, encouraging, and accessible no matter where you are in your development as a storyteller. The book presents a 'call to action' for writers to roll up their sleeves and begin, or to launch a rewrite with greater focus and clarity. But most importantly, it challenges writers to view the tools as a jumping off point to grow and shape your own process. Because **mastering your own process is the road to great writing.** That's empowering. That's the adventure. That's the journey that is the destination. That is being a writer.

Screenwriting as a form, is an applied art, or a craft, that is used to set up what becomes the actual final telling of your story: the film. But it begins with you and the story you're about to create.

"To make a fine film you need three things:
a great script, a great script, and a great script."
~ Alfred Hitchcock

Storytelling has a ton of guides, format, and structure governing how they are presented and designed. These structures create a framework for you to focus your themes and characters.

Think of the craft as a set of tools to shape your ideas. Like a stone carver and his tools, you need to master your writer tools so that they not only don't get in the way of your story, but they actually set it free.

"I saw the angel in the marble
and carved until I set it free."
~ Michelangelo

A screenplay has no excess. You will carve away anything that doesn't serve the story. But first, you have to build it.

What's presented in this book is a working-process without fluff. It's a straightforward, step-by-step, writer's process.

Without a doubt you can get from idea to finished story with this process as is, but I urge you to use this process as a starting point for developing your own process.

Learn this process, master the skills and then add to them, modify them, subtract pieces, and adjust pieces to fit how you work. Master artists make their tools and materials too. That's part of their secret to successfully creating great works.

I urge you to make learning an active part of your process too. Develop your craft of story design so that it becomes seamless to you. Do that, and you can bring your ideas to life with pure emotional impact. The goal is to effortlessly process your inspiration through the mechanics of your craft, deliver your story to an audience with clarity and heart, and hopefully inspire them the way you were inspired.

Master the craft so you can set free the art inside you.

HOW TO USE THIS BOOK

THIS IS AN ACTION-ORIENTED BOOK. That means you should be taking action to write your story along with the steps presented in the coming pages.

If you're a new writer, this book is going to provide you with all of the pieces needed to create a story. It'll guide you in building a story meant for scripting a feature screenplay (or even writing a novel). If you're a more seasoned writer and maybe you've read a dozen or more books, took some seminars, maybe even graduated from a writing program, this process is going to take those pieces you already have, reinforce them, put them in a good working order, and then fill in the blanks so that your process will be complete.

Since the information in this book is an actual writer's process, you should work with it from start to finish the first time. Then use it in the future as a reference guide by jumping to whatever sections you need. Each chapter offers tools you can use over and over from building the first draft through any stage of your rewrites. They'll help you discover problems in scenes or structure, and guide you in reforming elements of your story to make them work better. Even if you just now came to this process with a first draft already finished and ready to rewrite, you can use the tools to unearth problems and learn how to fix them.

And in the immortal words of one of my mentors, 'If you have a better solution, then use it.' Use what you know. If you have answers that work better for you, then by all means don't discard them. And you don't have to throw away what you'll learn here either. The last time I checked, a carpenter has more than one tool to accomplish any one task.

Before you begin, you should get a notebook or start a file on your computer that is designated as your 'story journal'. This is where you'll keep track of all your work for the story you're going to write. Every time you start a new story, start a new journal.

Fall in love with the process.

Treat writing and storytelling like it's something you love. Give that care and attention to every facet of your work, from the journal you keep, to the seat you sit in, to the choices you make for your characters and story, and to yourself as you take the journey and do the work. Take your time with things, care for it.

Along with setting up your story journal, try to designate a specific time every day to work. Rhythm and consistency spark the creative mind. Prepare your workspace with a good chair, maybe things that inspire you like figurines or pictures. And set an amount of time you will work so that you get used to measuring your own progress. You should tell others that this time is sacred as well, you need uninterrupted focus.

I also advise you to not talk about your work while it's fresh. That has a way of killing the subconscious and defusing your ideas. Let ideas live in your head until you complete a full first draft.

If you follow along through all the steps you'll definitely get to the finish-line with everything you need to write your script. And believe me, that's more than half the battle already won. Once you have your story designed, the Dynamic Dialogue and Description chapter will help guide you straight into your scripting choices.

I urge you to **trust the process**. You'll see that stated again and again throughout this book like a mantra. Many things in this process will be repeated so that you'll remember, but more importantly so you'll see how the story-building elements are intertwined and feed future steps. Trust the structure and the rules and guides because they will advance your knowledge of storytelling and make the entire writing process more fun and more fulfilling.

Writing and storytelling is truly a journey. It's going to teach you as much about yourself, as you learn about storytelling or the story you're writing. In time, if you're anything like me, your writing journey will intertwine with your life journey and that's when the magic really happens.

I know you can get there. So trust the process, and yourself.

Now get yourself ready, and take the leap into the next step...

"THE MOST HONEST FORM OF FILMMAKING IS TO **MAKE A FILM FOR YOURSELF.**"

- PETER JACKSON

BAD TASTE
DEAD ALIVE
HEAVENLY CREATURES
THE FRIGHTENERS
THE LORD OF THE RINGS: 1,2,3
KING KONG (2005)
THE HOBBIT: 1,2,3
THE LOVELY BONES
MORTAL ENGINES

CHAPTER 1
WHAT TO WRITE, OR: IT CAME IN THROUGH THE BATHROOM WINDOW

LET'S TALK ABOUT IDEAS**...** *and* get ready to work. Ideas are strange little buggers. They're plentiful, but elusive. In the beginning they can seem brilliant in one moment, and stupid in the next. They can lead you boldly into sudden dead ends and fade away like ghosts at dawn. Shine a little light on one... gone. Look straight at it... gone. They act a little like trying to put smoke in a bottle.

But believe it or not, that's not an impossible task.

Our goal here is to pick an idea that you trust, get you to believe in it beyond yourself, and then develop it into something strong enough to go the distance.

YOU ARE YOUR FIRST AUDIENCE >>>>>

First... Hey, you in the back! Shut up, we're talkin' about ideas here, and it's important! Don't be skipping ahead either!

So listen, you don't want to get stuck in the middle of nowhere, or the middle of writing Act 2, when your idea dries up suddenly and you feel like throwing yourself off a cliff. Oh, believe me, you will feel like quitting during your writing journey. But, process is going to save your butt and get you to the Promised Land.

And I wasn't telling some imaginary kid in the back of class to pipe down a second ago; I'm talking to that voice in the back of your head that wants to rush in and just start writing. Because that's the same voice that will urge you to quit later and try to convince you that you don't know s#!t.

It's better to grab that doubting voice by the throat right now.

Whether you've stepped into this storytelling journey with your idea already in hand, or you're still hunting for a subject to write about, the first step in your creative process has already begun. All creative work is a process, and it begins with searching your own heart and having an open mind (without a critic in the back).

Ask yourself: what do I love about my favorite movies?

Your answer identifies the invisible force that points your unique artist compass to true north.

Yeah, yeah... sounds wishy washy, right? But what in the heck are you doing this for anyway? What made you want to write stories in the first place? What adventure do you want to take? Or take others on? The answer is elusive, right?

Maybe some movie you watched pulled you out of time, made you feel romantic about something or someone, or excited, or scared, or introspective. Maybe you're writing a personal story you lived. But the spark is always a feeling. That's where it begins, and the answer to that first question about what you love, is only for you.

It's a personal answer and it doesn't matter what anyone else thinks... *At least not yet.*

But, chasing a feeling around in the dark hoping to materialize your vision is a recipe for failure, or at the very least insane amounts of frustration. Mighty writers have abandoned projects because they launched an idea without a plan. Writing is a journey, with copious amounts of discovery. Some paths are well known. But most paths you're going to have to venture onto by yourself.

So, knowing your heart is like providing yourself with a compass. *Get it? Journey... compass.* Okay, okay, you get it.

Take some time with this concept though. Seriously. Get out your story journal and write down what you love about your favorite movies or books. Get specific. Narrow it down. There are no right or wrong answers. Were they heroic adventures? A heart-wrenching love story? Scared you until you had to turn off the sound and hide under a pillow? Was it inspirational? Did you cry? Maybe laughed until you cried? Underdog story?

Write what you love.

The point is to recognize what *specifically* gets your attention and moves you. And equally important, by examining this you've tiptoed over the line to look at stories and movies objectively, like a writer. Although, just barely. You did it by identifying elements that stood out so strongly in a story that they grabbed you. Now you can examine those things. Aim for them. Emulate them. And soon, we're going to do exactly that.

This is some left-brain / right-brain stuff. Part analysis, part emotion; head and heart. You're going to need both as a writer. And you will constantly jump back and forth between them.

A side note: if you ever find yourself lost in your story, or lost in your career, come back to this. It's a touchstone, and it'll instantly aim you back in the right direction. Maybe help you re-focus your initial idea. Or it might take you straight back to that plot point you're struggling with, but then help you choose between options and design your solutions.

Your compass is an idea finder, but also a block breaker.

EXPANDING YOUR VISION >>>>>

Wherever you're at with your idea right now, know that thinking objectively about what inspires you to write has put you another step closer to realizing your story.

Congratulations! You're already moving forward.

Now we're going to lock down a few core ideas and begin to fill your story world with a tangible vision.

INTUITION AND THE WRITER

Before we start swinging at our foggy ideas like blind fools, let's pause a second and have a chat about **intuition**.

Intuition is a convergence of all your senses, it includes your intellect, and a lot of unseen variables you're not aware of.

Combined, the facets of your intuition form the force compelling you toward something. It's the flicker of a feeling that makes you decide to smell a flower. It's the unrecognized urge that makes you gravitate to one movie poster over another, you might say, 'just because.'

We all have intuition. We use it all of the time to make choices. The only thing that gets in the way is when we try to overthink it. Don't. Overthinking is the critic in the back whose about to get kicked out of class!

Follow your intuition... it's always right.

Intuition is where art lives. 'Flow states' exist there. It dances between the left and right brain, drawing on both, but relying on neither. And guess what? You already used it by identifying your inspiration.

Why all this talk about intuition? Because it's one of the most important tools any writer can use. As artists/writers, it's our job to constantly go where no one has gone before. Which means you won't have a map. No one can tell you if your choices are correct because your intuition is unique to you and focused by your intentions. It's your gut. It's essential that you trust yourself and trust your choices.

So let's give it a try by consciously guiding some solid, left-brain choices, that will bolster your right-brain idea.

Now, I'm not so thickheaded as to believe you don't already have some notion of what you want to create. I'll bet you came to this with something already burning your brain. A favorite movie, love story, true story, social topic, family vacation, or maybe you just want to watch stuff explode.

But, something got you this far.

So, let's zoom in a little by making one assumption: **along with your subject, you also know the genre your writing in.** Got one in mind? If not, here's your chance.

Complete the following sentence in your story journal:

I am writing a ***insert your genre*** story,
about ***insert your subject***.

For example:

I am writing a ***drama*** story,
about ***climbing Mt. Everest***.

That simple sentence is like your North Star. Don't worry about it being perfect. There is no such thing as perfection. Besides, imperfections and holes are simply opportunities to create and improve. So, stay loose because in coming chapters we'll revisit this and really lock it down.

Right now, it's time for a field trip!

"**YOU HAVE TO DO TONS OF RESEARCH,** BECAUSE YOU DON'T KNOW WHERE THE **INSPIRATION** IS GOING TO COME FROM."

- JOHN LASSETER

TOY STORY
CARS
A BUG'S LIFE
MONSTERS INC.
FINDING NEMO
BEAUTY AND THE BEAST
RATATOUILLE
THE INCREDIBLES
WALL-E
FROZEN
ZOOTOPIA
MOANA

CHAPTER 2
CREATIVE RESEARCH: DOWN THE RABBIT HOLE

THE GOAL WITH CREATIVE RESEARCH is to solidify your feelings and impulses by gathering visual elements in support of your raw idea. With these images you'll begin to **form the vision** for your story and make your idea real.

With your story journal in hand, start hunting for images, movies, books, magazines, or comics that reflect the style you think is relevant to your idea. You're looking for the cool factor. Emotional resonance. Anything that moves you or draws a second glance, save it, because that's intuition at work.

Explore, but with purpose.

Let your intuition guide you, but float nearby in your mind like an objective observer. Write down ideas that pop in your head. Make sketches. Save your selected images to an image file for the film you're about to write. *We'll revisit that file later.*

Shape your growing vision by selecting photos of possible settings for your film, or favorite actors that you might cast, a product or prop you want to include, a costume, buildings, or vehicles with particular style or period. Might be an image or color swatch that simply defines the mood and color pallet you envision. Anything that might belong in your genre-specific story world.

Go farther and immerse yourself. Are you considering writing that story about climbing Mt. Everest? Go hike a mountain. Buy climbing gear. Take notes. Write down how it feels. What did you hear and smell and taste and touch? Take a piece of mountain home, put it on your writing desk. Find images of what you saw that are stylized to fit your genre and growing mental picture of your idea. Set your imagination loose!

Be an active observer.

Remember those ideas way back that seemed like they could disappear simply by looking at them? Well, now you have visuals. Like capturing a ghost on film. **Your idea is becoming real. You can reference the images, cultivate your vision, and see with your own eyes what was previously only in your head.**

By the time you're done, you've filled your imagination with all sorts of stuff to populate your story world later. You've zeroed in on movies and stories that were made. And you're probably looking at your favorite movies and stories more objectively.

With that, you bolstered your idea, proved that it can be done, and started building a **concept**, one that you can believe in (and see.)

MINI ASSIGNMENT >>>>>

Before you leave this creative leg of your research, you have one specific, objective task that will sharpen your focus.

Pick your favorite movie that is related to what you're considering writing. Watch it with your story journal in hand and write down the following five things about it:

1. Name of the movie and its primary genre(s).
2. In 30 words or less, state what the story is about.
3. In as few words as possible, identify the #1 most important thing that the protagonist wants.
4. What or who is the main source of opposition?
5. Did the protagonist get what they wanted by the end of the movie? Was getting it (or not getting it) good or bad?

Here's an example. It's an oldie but a goodie...

Steven Spielberg's, **'JAWS'**:

1. *JAWS. Adventure-thriller.*
2. *A small beach town's sheriff must hunt down a huge man-eating shark before it eats more people in his town.*
3. *He wants to save his family and community by killing the shark.*
4. *The shark.*
5. *Yes, he got what he wanted. It was good because he faced his fears and saved his community.*

Okay, ready to get serious? Yeah, me neither. Remember to have fun with your writing or nobody else will when they read your story. I guarantee that even Ted Tally had fun writing Hannibal Lector for 'SILENCE OF THE LAMBS'. He's deliciously evil. Hannibal...not Ted. Am I right? And now Dr. Lector and his fava beans have become legendary cinema lexicon. I wonder what Ted's research was like.

By now your idea should be forming pretty clearly in your head. It doesn't have a plot yet, or structure, or characters. In fact, it's probably still an amorphous blob. But one with tone and texture and color and purpose and visuals. I imagine you're feeling pretty good about it. And you should.

Up until now, we've been focusing on you and your artistic interests. Ultimately we're going to return to that for the duration of the book, because this is about how to write a story. But as writers crafting an applied art project, we need to look farther afield than our own interests for a minute.

We need to take a look at the market with analytical left-brain objectivity. It may not sound fun, but it'll separate the players from the wannabes. And by the time you're done, you'll be ready.

WRITE TO MARKET >>>>>

'Writing to market' refers to the concept of customizing your story to the target audience you're hoping to reach.

There are two ways to examine the write to market concept.

1. SHOW ME THE MONEY

The first way to view 'write to market' is by simply seeing what types of stories/movies are currently selling.

In other words, is there a genre that's hot right now that everyone wants to see? This is a little bit deceiving when considering a project to launch because by the time you're finished writing it, the market may have cooled and moved on to something different.

Gimme the same thing, only different.

You can definitely learn something about the zeitgeist of the moment and what audiences are responding to by identifying what's hot and selling. So don't shun the box office reports. Something about those successful movies drew people to them! And if they're big enough (AVATAR), then they're going to be **genre-shaping** stories worth taking a closer look at.

2. TROPES AND ROPES

THE SCREENWRITER'S WAY is designed for your creative development, which leads us to the second way of understanding how to *write to market:* **the identification of what creative elements are unique to the stories you're going to write.**

Trope:

A significant or recurrent theme; a motif.

This is a creative way of analyzing films and stories. Basically, looking for those recurrent themes, guidelines, formats, character archetypes, props, and settings that your genre typically embodies.

Sort of like those guys in the horror/comedy movie 'SCREAM' talking about the rules of surviving a horror movie:

- *You may not survive the movie if you have sex.*
- *You may not survive the movie if you drink or do drugs.*
- *You may not survive the movie if you say, "I'll be right back", "Hello?" or "Who's there?"*

That example is a little tongue-in-cheek. But it illustrates the idea.

FINAL EXERCISE >>>>>

Pick at least three films/stories (could be a book too) that you feel successfully embody the kind of story you want to tell, and are within your genre. They could be your personal favorites since you're likely a fan of the genre you want to write. They could be historical heavyweights in a genre like, 'LORD OF THE RINGS' or 'THE GODFATHER'. Maybe it's a story from the hottest new writer or director to hit your genre scene like 'NOPE' or 'NOMADLAND'.

While you're watching them, take note of tropes similarly represented in all of them. Watch how their stories unfold and how character or plot decisions are made at certain keys points of the protagonist's journey. Do the movies you're comparing all have similar outcomes for the hero? Write it down.

The goal is to find things that audiences respond to and expect from the genres they love. You can use those things to earn their trust as you unfold your story. You can also go against the grain and surprise an audience, but you have to know how to do that.

This knowledge will carry a boatload of great stuff over to the next chapter when you nail down your idea, especially the **setting**.

LAST WORD

As you continue to develop your story, remember that nothing is sacred. You can throw out anything, even your own favorite work.

You, as artist, must develop your own internal barometer about what people respond to and what connects you to them, because you want to communicate emotion to them.

That's your true task. That's the 'business of being an artist'.

We'll revisit this idea again before we're finished.

"**NEVER SAY NO TO AN IDEA.** YOU NEVER KNOW HOW THAT IDEA WILL IGNITE ANOTHER IDEA."

- STANLEY KUBRICK

A KILLERS KISS
PATHS OF GLORY
SPARTACUS
LOLITA
2001: A SPACE ODYSSEY
A CLOCKWORK ORANGE
DR. STRANGELOVE
THE SHINING
FULL METAL JACKET
EYES WIDE SHUT

CHAPTER 3

CAPTURE AND MAGNIFY YOUR STORY IDEA

BAM! INSPIRATION hit you like a bolt of lightning. A story idea lit up your brain! You saw images, characters and scenes, all the jumps, cuts, and connective tissue racing through your mind make total sense. It could be brilliant! You're sure that audiences will laugh, and cry, and love what you created...

But the second you put pen to paper (or tap a keyboard) and you try to develop your new idea, it seems to break apart like a dream upon waking. It stops making sense.

You don't know where to take it or where your protagonist wants to go. And, who's the protagonist, anyway? Frustration sets in. Pretty soon, you're lost, or worse...you abandon the idea and quit.

No need to quit now! Not after your field trip. However, your idea is still without form. It's undefined and in danger of falling apart.

Great stories are built.

Stories are complex and have defined structure. Your ideas are only the beginning, and until you define and refine them, they're as hard to grasp as a puff of smoke in the wind. They're sensitive and elusive because they're mostly emotion at the outset.

So if you're going to capture your 'lightning in a bottle' idea, you should adopt the philosophy that stories are built step-by-step.

Stories surely don't spring out of our minds fully formed and ready. If you've ever seen that from some writer in the movies, feverishly typing out every last detail in a stream of consciousness… I hate to say it, but that only happens in the movies.

What you will learn from this chapter is how to use six simple steps to build an initial framework around your fresh, and probably still nebulous, idea. From that initial framework, you will then expand your newly solidified idea to create a full story plan. With plan in hand, you can then launch confidently into writing your script.

Some of these initial steps may seem so simple that you can simply skip them. You shouldn't. When you do the foundation work your writing experience will be more fun, more fulfilling, and will set you free to expand your creativity.

I said that before, but it bears repeating. And let's not forget your writer's mantra:

Trust the process.

These following six steps begin shaping the storytelling process. It should also begin to make you more process-oriented in doing all creative work. So, capturing your idea in this way will be your first solid building block in more ways than one; part for your story, and partly for you...*writer*. And with your hands solidly around a plan *that you create*, you are in far better shape to actually finish your story.

Without a plan, writing a story is like pushing a bowling ball through a garden hose. You ain't gettin' far! And just as important, with a clearly defined initial idea, the chances that your screenplay will be clearer, more powerful, and more compelling increases dramatically.

By the time you finish this chapter you will have your hands firmly around the story you're going to tell.

THE CREATIVE PROCESS >>>>>

To drive your creativity, and keep you on course, I first want to introduce you to a few concepts that will help you stay with your idea as you go through the six idea-building steps.

THE BOX

Imagination happens outside the box. It's free and goes in any direction it wants; uncontrolled and unfocused, and it's wonderful. It's a child at play, it's you at your most free.

But, contrary to popular belief; **creativity** happens INSIDE the box. The box is made of constraints that you decide and place on your idea in order to focus it.

The box and its constraints invite creativity. In fact, if you are going to take the full journey of your story, these constraints will *demand* you become more creative. And remember the secret: true masters know how to define the rules, build their tools, AND create the art within it.

Embrace the constraints you will create, beginning with the six steps I am introducing you to next. Like many things in this book, I'll start simply, then repeat and build on the concepts.

So first, a basic list of the steps to get you thinking:

1. **Choose a genre.**
2. **Decide on a setting.**
3. **Clarify your subject.**
4. **Create your protagonist.**
5. **Design the antagonist.**
6. **Choose the ending of the story.**

If you find yourself feeling a little lost or unsure while unfolding your story, you can return to the box of constraints you'll be defining in a moment. Through repeated refinement, you'll refocus yourself and ignite your creativity again.

Remember, the creative box is yours to create, and it acts as your touchstone while you head into the unknown.

So as you boldly go where no one has gone before, to discover something that no one else has before, you're going to test the outer borders of what you know best. That might make you uneasy. The anxious sensation of testing the edge and walking into the murky unknown, might feel like worry. That's where even great artists can start doubting themselves or their ideas…

That feeling is natural. So stay with it! Embrace it.

Creativity takes courage.

The fact is if you don't have that feeling of unease, you may only be treading the same creative ground that you always have (or someone else has) and you need to push the bounds of your creativity a little more. When you're feeling afraid of failing, or like you don't know where to go, you have to summon the courage to follow your idea and trust your creative constraints to lead you safely to new ground.

Your vulnerability is the gateway to that courage you need. Loving your story, your idea, and your craft will give you the power to move forward into your courage.

That's when creative breakthroughs happen!

That's also the hero's journey you are about to embark on with your protagonist. So if you're not willing to go into the unknown by finding courage, then how will they?

THE WRITER'S JOURNEY

Making choices is the writer's primary task. You'll endlessly make choices about everything in your story, right down to the exact word a character says when you write their dialogue. You'll weigh all of these smaller choices against the set up and design of characters, plot structure, scenes design and more. It all links together like a web; pull one thread and it pulls another. So it's very important you make lucid, logical choices along the way.

Mushy decision-making will come back to haunt you.

Ultimately, you're making choices as the overlord of your story's world, so that your characters will make the dramatic choices you want them to make. Thus, expressing your narrative intent. That means, the story gets told with emotional truth and conviction. That's what makes audiences laugh, cry, and learn, and love you.

THE SIX STEPS >>>>>

The following six steps for defining your idea are designed to initiate a creative narrowing process called convergence, and they will guide you in how to develop your keystone story choices.

Doing these first steps in the process will laser focus your story idea and demand even more of your creativity.

So, let's go!

STEP 1. CHOOSE A GENRE

Picking a genre for your story is like putting a giant floor under your idea. Someplace to plant your feet.

As a foundation, each genre provides a unique field to play on and introduces distinct rules to govern your choices of setting, subject, character, and more.

Genre is another word for 'category'.

Horror, Sci-fi, Romantic-comedy, Comedy, Drama, etc., are all genres. Some stories will demand a specific genre, like a true war story. Otherwise the choice is yours.

A word of caution:
Be specific and avoid too many hyphenate genres.

For example: *action-horror-comedy.*

Hyphenates dilute your idea and dull its power, making it harder to understand the dominating tones and rules for your story. Hyphenates are not taboo, but the clearer you are, the stronger your idea and story will be.

Study the rules of your chosen genre, because they come with promises to an audience and specific demands for your creativity. Genre also provides a general toolbox and materials to build your story with.

So select your genre. (You should have done this earlier with the first exercise. A little cheat to seed your creative ground.) Write it down now. *Step 1 is an easy one.*

STEP 2. DECIDE ON A SETTING

Your setting defines two things: space and time.

Selecting a setting begins the process of turning your idea into a three-dimensional concept. Like the wall of a box built on your genre foundation, setting first acts like a backdrop on a stage you're building. It defines location(s), and it's the start of world-building.

A setting's location is the physical environment where your story unfolds.

Genre and setting work together to define your story's domain. But while genre defines rules and tones, the physical aspect of setting defines objects and places. It can be as big as Pandora in 'AVATAR', or as small as the room in 'ROOM'.

Settings are not passive.

Settings are active and influence characters' choices. Just like the characters inhabiting them, settings are alive and change and evolve. They have attitude and are filled with three-dimensional 'stuff' to give your world scale and engage your protagonist while they make choices that will shape their character.

These things include: genre specific props, buildings, vehicles, and landscape. *Imagine Tom Hanks in 'CASTAWAY' escaping a desert island vs. Luke Skywalker escaping the Deathstar in 'STAR WARS'... those settings have very different things populating them for your characters to interact with.*

Choices define character.

Different story worlds provide different options available for characters and demand unique choices. How they move through their world of choices illustrates who they are and how they change.

For example: *Is your protagonist a meek factory worker in a horribly oppressive non-union factory, because you want to explore the American labor movement? Is he an innocent man imprisoned in the cruelest prison ever, because you want to explore a man's will to survive? Is she a teenager struggling to survive a murderous madman in a suburban neighborhood, because you want to play with modern psychological customs? Or is he a high school slacker who just wants to surf, because you're telling a fun story about youth?*

TIME PERIOD >>>>>

The second aspect that magnifies setting is the time period of your story. Is it set in the past or present? Old west? Future? Medieval? Also, what time of year; winter, summer, etc? Like location, time period also dictates a lot of physical story elements for characters to overcome that you need to consider.

So jot down your specific time period, along with the physical location, and we'll plow onward.

But first, while we're talking about time...

TIMEFRAME

Timeframe is the amount of time that passes from beginning to end during your story. You don't need to know this yet, we'll revisit it when we build your structure. But it's good to start thinking about this for reasons of pace and scope.

So, looking at what you've done already by declaring your genre and setting, do you see the linkage between them? Because the same way genre is linked to setting, setting links to subject.

STEP 3. CLARIFY YOUR SUBJECT

Your subject is probably self-evident. That means you already have it close to your heart because it's where your idea began. It was your first impulse and interest.

Subject is what your story is about.

For example you might want to tell a true story about political corruption, or about the inspiration of falling in love as a teenager, or about first contact with aliens, or maybe about the tough life of a boxer.

But after steps one and two, you should now have a genre floor under your subject providing basic rules, and a setting to give it scale; both helping you define your subject better. Imagine the difference between 'E.T.' (Sci-fi/adventure set in suburban Earth) and 'ALIENS' (Sci-fi/horror set on a hostile planet). Different genres, different settings, with similar subjects (alien first contact). Those first two choices equate to radically different stories.

Now, to further clarify your subject, you need to create 'travel' for the characters from one condition to another. To do that you need to:

Polarize the conditions.

There needs to be good or evil, scarcity or abundance, weak or strong, etc., in your protagonist's world at the outset of the story in order to give it direction. Because your hero is going to move from one through to the other.

For example: *Is boxing brutal and destructive (ROCKY), or an art form for heroes (ALI)? Does finding love erupt from loneliness or from come as a challenge born of confidence (HITCH)?*

From the film: 'ROCKY'. A down and out, past his prime boxer gets a once in a lifetime shot to fight the world heavyweight champion for the title. << *Each of those aspects is polarized.*

Like it or not, 'ROCKY' sets the stage for enormous protagonist travel. That means HUGE transformation. In 1977, audiences were literally cheering in the theaters for Rocky to beat Apollo during the final climactic fight! That's because his journey was enormous and the stakes were huge, as defined by how polarized his story world was at the outset.

Once you have polarized conditions, they will then be put off balance to set the stage for conflict as your protagonist travels through your world. (i.e. A shy teenager sees the girl of his dreams. A peaceful life interrupted by war. Safety invaded by evil.)

Look at 'AVATAR', 'STAR WARS', 'THELMA AND LOUISE', 'GET OUT', or 'ROOM'. All illustrated strongly polarized beginnings that forced protagonists forward through conflict.

Polarization sets the stage for conflict.

CONFLICT IS KING!

Take a minute and write a sentence or two about your subject. Use at that example from 'Rocky' to help you. Keep it simple, clean and clear.

Clarifying your subject with step 3 just added another wall to your box: **depth**. It will set up your story's perspective.

STEP 4. CREATE YOUR PROTAGONIST

Genre, setting, and subject have set up the world your protagonist will travel through. He or she (or *it*... could be a robot (WALL-E)) is the key to your story.

Protagonist is your hero or main character.

The protagonist springs up automatically in relationship to the subject. They will start at one end of your polarized conditions. The direction they travel will define your story's point of view. *(i.e. - good will defeat evil if they believe in the force. Luke Skywalker.)*

So we need to set your protagonist within your world at a place that will demand action (travel). Here's how...

The #1 most important thing you need to know about your protagonist is also going to be the #1 most important driving force of your entire story.

This is the dramatic want.

DRAMATIC WANT >>>>>

What one thing does your protagonist ***want*** *more than anything?*

The 'dramatic want' sets your hero in place in your world. It will drive him/her and define his/her opposition. It's at the heart of your subject, it will define all the major plot points, influence any scene he/she is in and many they are not, and determine the ending of your story.

Basically, everything hinges on this dramatic want.

Obviously this is highest priority. So make the protagonist's dramatic 'want' specific. Very specific. Make it important. And link it to your subject.

For example: *'JAWS'. A small town sheriff must hunt down a man-eating shark in order to protect the town and his family. *Protecting his family and the town is his dramatic want.)*

Here are a few notable protagonists and their wants:

- *Frodo in 'Lord of the Rings': To save the shire and his friends.*
- *Luke Skywalker: To defeat the empire and avenge his family.*
- *Elle in 'Legally Blonde': To win the man of her dreams.*
- *Solomon in '12 Years A Slave': To escape slavery.*
- *Wesley in 'A Princess Bride': To rescue his true love.*

**Heroes will stop at nothing, even challenging death itself, to attain their dramatic want.*

In the course of designing your protagonist (or any character), the dramatic want is their core. There's much more you'll take into consideration before your hero is full-bodied and ready to live and breathe, like their inner and outer needs.

But you don't need to know those just yet, because right now we are only fleshing out your idea. We'll get into 'needs' more extensively in the bio chapter. So, it's good to have your protagonist's needs on your radar.

INNER NEEDS come from a place of personal lack. A thing each character is missing inside, like courage, trust, or belief in self.

OUTER NEEDS come in the form of the physical thing they need to overcome in order to capture their dramatic want; like learning to box, or drive a race car, or kill a shark.

WRITE IT UP >>>>>

For now, pencil in what you know. Is your protagonist a man or woman? Their name? Age? Profession? Just write down what you know now. But most importantly, define their dramatic want. Your hero would stop at nothing in order to get this one thing.

All you need for now is your version of this:

> ***'Wizard of Oz'***
> ***Protagonist**: Dorothy, 11, Kansas farm girl*
> ***Dramatic want**: to find home.*

Now, let's put some roadblocks in our hero's path…

STEP 5. DESIGN THE ANTAGONIST

Every hero needs a villain. The antagonist acts as a catalyst for the protagonist to change by being the embodiment of opposition to the protagonist's dramatic want. They do this by presenting obstacles, specifically chosen by you, to force your hero to choose… and thereby change and grow.

Antagonism can come from a group of bad guys like the Nazi's, or it can come from the forces of nature like an impassable desert, or it can even come from within the protagonist themselves due to a serious flaw like alcoholism or gambling addiction.

But, for the sake of clarity and learning we are going to view the antagonist as an individual for now. *(FYI: Even if you have a group as your force of antagonism, likely there is one within the group that stands out as the leader.)*

One of my screenwriting mentors used to say, in regards to antagonists:

'One shark is better than two barracuda'.

Or in the immortal words of the Mayor in the movie 'JAWS':

"You yell barracuda, everybody says, 'Huh? What?'
You yell shark, we've got a panic on our hands on the
Fourth of July."

In other words, the antagonist should be the biggest, baddest, scariest fish in the sea. And you want people to panic when they walk in the room. They may have help in the form of henchmen, even legions of henchmen like the Stormtroopers. But, the antagonist must be the most formidable, most ruthless, most vile, harshest, son-of-a-bitch around (Darth Vader).

This opposing force needs to be an obstacle so difficult to defeat that it will take every ounce of what your hero can muster, and all the things he/she learns on their journey, to overcome the antagonist and claim the prize.

Antagonists and protagonists are eternally linked in the world of your story. They're yin and yang; each is a champion of one end of your polarized subject.

It's a good time to remember that:

>>> *CONFLICT IS KING!* <<<

Antagonists are designed based on the wants of the protagonist. If your hero is doubtful (Jerry Maguire), the villain should be confident and will probably exploit the hero's doubts. If the hero is weak (Rocky's boxing skills), the villain might be strong (a perfect pugilist like Apollo Creed) and just simply muscle the hero under.

Whatever the protagonist wants to get more than anything, the antagonist has the tools, and the will, to block his/her success.

A word of caution:

The antagonist must be ACTIVE.

Design your villain to oppose the protagonist, but make him/her as full-bodied, complete, and self-directed as the hero. In fact, they have their own version of a dramatic want, and it will likely be either in direct opposition to the hero, or be the same dramatic want as the hero, but for different reasons.

For example: *Darth Vader is one of the most perfect antagonists of all time. He was pure evil. But he didn't think he was evil. In fact, he thought he was doing 'good' by saving the galaxy, and he had an agenda that he acted on with or without Luke's want. Vader's actions were however, designed to oppose the hero, Luke Skywalker's actions.*

It was inevitable that they would clash.

Here are a few notable antagonists and how they were designed to oppose the hero:

- ***Hannibal Lector*** *in 'Silence of the Lambs': FBI Agent Clarice Starling was pure and fresh and seeking truth. Lector was devious and deceptive and evil. Both were trying to find a serial killer.*
- ***Apollo Creed*** *in 'Rocky': Rocky was a brute and not smart, but he was all heart. Whereas Apollo was refined, brilliant, an artist of boxing. Both wanted to win the heavyweight title.*
- ***The Shark*** *in 'Jaws': Chief Brody was fair, loving, and noble. The shark was relentless, mindless, savage. They would battle over the lives of the townspeople.*
- ***Darth Vader*** *in 'Star Wars': Luke Skywalker is virtuous, innocent, and courageous. But Vader, literally in all black*

and shrouded in machinery, is pure evil. Heartless, cold, brutal and also relentless. One wants to rule the galaxy, the other wants to set it free.

Great antagonists make for great stories.

Without a massively formidable antagonist, your story will be boring and flat. Your hero won't be forced to face their deepest fears and challenge their physical limits. They won't grow, and without that arc of growth, your audience will learn nothing and won't care.

So, same as your protagonist, sketch out what you know already about your antagonist. Name, race, occupation, and their dramatic want. Get the basics, consider your genre, subject, setting, and protagonist's want. Soon, you'll write a full bio for your villain.

I'll let you in on a secret, likely you'll learn more about your story's plot by writing the antagonist's bio than anything else. It's because your antagonist is going to present a lot of obstacles and ignite A LOT of conflict from their own wants and actions.

The conflict will come in the form of physical, mental, and emotional obstacles. Overcoming what the antagonist dishes out will shape the character of your hero *(and it's interesting to watch.)*

I urge you to be as relentless with designing your villain as you can. Spare nothing. Go all the way and farther. Design them to seem unbeatable. Call forth your audience's worst nightmare

Oddly enough, as a writer, you will love your villain for being so bad! *(queue sinister laugh)*

Now write it up the same way you did for the protagonist.

STEP 6. CHOOSE THE ENDING OF YOUR STORY

THE END? Already? Yup. Now you have to decide if your protagonist will get the thing he/she wants more than anything, and how that happens.

Starting with the end in mind provides you with a clear destination, a path to take, suggests obstacles, and clues you in to the tools, supplies, and companions your hero will need to complete their journey. By the time you reach your chosen ending you need to wrap up all the loose plot lines, and you can't do that without knowing when and how the end will come.

Choosing your ending also caps off the box of constraints encapsulating your idea. That should make you feel strong, because it gives you a solid foundation to build on.

But before you choose your ending, let's recap your idea:

1. **Genre** gave you thematic rules and a toolbox to build with.
2. **Setting** gave you a scale, a world, and stuff to fill it with. It includes time period and the inkling of a timeframe.
3. **Subject** ignited your idea, but it now has specificity and polarized conditions to provide depth and perspective.
4. **Protagonist** is on a side and has a dramatic want that they will do anything to get and demands transformation (travel) to get it.

5. **Antagonist** will oppose the protagonist with active measures toward achieving his/her own plans, and everything they do elevates conflict.

You'll want to nail your ending down, but, don't worry if you don't know all the details yet. The ending is a mountaintop under your North Star. There's a lot of writer's journey remaining before all of your story is hammered out.

For now, what does your gut tell you about your ending? What do you envision? Does the romantic hero punch the bad guy in the face and win the girl? Do they win the big race in a wild, edge of your seat finish? Or do they lose the big race? Do they save the world by throwing the one ring into Mt. Doom? Do they escape the island in a one way, death defying expedition? You get the idea.

Bottom line, does your protagonist get what they set out to get, and how will it happen? Keep it simple, but definitely choose. You may adjust things later, which brings up another undeniable writer axiom:

Writing is rewriting.

BEGINNINGS AND ENDINGS >>>>>

Now that you've taken aim at your chosen ending, here's a trick that will help you begin your plot when we get into structure: knowing where and how your story ends allows you to walk back in time and find the most suitable starting point. (Inciting incident; we'll go in the I.I. later.)

Think about beginning your story in a place as far from the hero achieving their goal as you can get, but still within the world of your subject and protagonist.

Your protagonist will probably be the polar opposite at the beginning from who they'll change into by the end in order to achieve their goal.

SUMMARY >>>>>

- *Great stories are built.*
- *Stories are all around you, all the time.*
- *Genre is just another word for 'category'.*
- *Be specific and avoid too many hyphenate genres.*
- *Setting is the physical environment where your story unfolds.*
- *Settings influence character's choices.*
- *Pick a setting that supports your subject.*
- *Subject is what your story about.*
- *Polarize the conditions.*
- *Conflict is King!*
- *Protagonist is your hero or main character.*
- *What does he want more than anything?*
- *Heroes prove your premise and central question.*
- *The antagonist is the opposition.*
- *The antagonist should be ACTIVE.*
- *Endings give rise to beginnings.*

STEP-BY-STEP IDEA BREAKDOWN >>>>>

The breakdown of your idea should be written down and expressed like the following six steps:

TITLE: 'TERMINATOR'

GENRE: Science Fiction/Action

SETTING: Present day Los Angeles. (Timeframe about 3-5 days)

SUBJECT: Intelligent, but murderous, machines want to exterminate humanity so they can take over the world.

PROTAGONIST: Sarah Conner, mid-20's, waitress, wants to escape a murderous robot so she can save her unborn son (the future leader of the human resistance to the machines).

ANTAGONIST: The T-800 Terminator, an unstoppable sentient robot that wants to kill Sarah to stop her son from becoming the leader of the resistance that will ultimately destroy the Terminators.

ENDING: Sarah destroys the T-800 in a one-on-one battle, and faces an uncertain future.

"I **BELIEVE,** WHATEVER DOESN'T KILL YOU, SIMPLY MAKES YOU... STRANGER."

- HEATH LEDGER

THE JOKER

CHAPTER 4

100 QUESTIONS TO CREATE GREAT CHARACTER BIOGRAPHIES

WHAT IS A CHARACTER BIO? >>>>>

A CHARACTER BIOGRAPHY is a personal profile of a fictional person. That person is going to be custom-shaped to illustrate your story premise/subject. They only become a 'character' after you've given them character traits, or personality.

character:
The mental and moral qualities
distinctive to an individual.

To build a dramatic character you need to build constraints for this fictional person, similar to how you did for your story idea. Even if your characters are based on real life people, you are still going to shape the way they're presented.

To do that you need to learn everything you can about your characters in order to bring them to life within the context and subject matter of your story.

The bios you'll write for each character will contain psychology, sociology, spirituality, and physiological aspects along with historical facts about the character's life that will have specific bearing on your story.

It can include anything that has been in your character's life since he or she was born. It will include things that happened before they were born too, all the way back to the beginning of time if it's relevant. It should definitely include his/her childhood, significant events in adolescence, formative events and influential people they met in later years.

It will even include defined gaps and holes, flaws and shortcomings. The bios are going to get intimate, because you, the writer, will know their deepest, darkest secrets.

A character bio is everything up to the beginning of your story when your audience meets them for the first time.

WHY SHOULD YOU WRITE BIOS? >>>>>

Stories are about characters. We often default to thinking of stories as being about plots and events. But plots and scenes are only vehicles designed to expose character and express the nature of their change through the choices they make when faced with a problem.

That brings up another great storytelling principle to etch in your writer's mind while designing your story:

Simple plot, complex characters.

Guaranteed you'll fight that one for awhile, because it's easy to solve story problems by throwing new events into the mix. But that's the equivalent of kicking the can down the road. After you work out a few plots, you'll see that complex plots overwhelm stories. Audiences are people, and they come to stories/movies to see how other people lived and solved problems.

Simple plot moments allow fuller expression of character choices, taking us into the details of their thinking and emotions, thus taking us deep.

A character bio is another form of creative framework. It keeps characters on track and helps determine how they will make choices. In fact, once you have a really full-bodied character, you can even give your character your narrative problems to solve...

You can't figure out why the protagonist entered a room? Have them decide. Don't know how they would handle a problem? Let them not know, until they figure it out.

Character choices determine plot outcomes.

In many cases, while shaping a bio, you'll discover things about characters that will change entire plot points. Some psychology about a hero that you didn't know at first glance might emerge and change the subtext or theme of a scene or a relationship with another character. As the writer, you're the master of this world, but at some point, you want to have fully realized characters that begin to speak and act without your guidance.

In other words, the more detailed and specific you are about your character's way of being, thinking, moving, and acting: the more he or she will show you where he/she wants to go.

For example: Can you imagine Forrest Gump suddenly making an intellectual choice to visit a library to research shrimp fishin' boats? No way! You know why? Because it wasn't in his *character; the nature of his being.*

WHO SHOULD GET A BIO? >>>>>

Start with your protagonist. This is the person that is going to carry the weight of your story and you will want to know more about him/her than anyone.

As you design other characters, like the antagonist, you will shape them to bring out aspects of the protagonist. But each should be as fully realized as possible. Avoid clichés and handy explanations you might have gotten from someplace else.

You should create a bio for all the leads: protagonist, antagonist, mentor, love interest. These are the major players and you should know them the best. After that, you should create a bio for every supporting character of significance: sidekicks, and main henchmen to the antagonist.

A significant character is one that will perform a specific service or function to your story that influences events.

Beyond them, you don't need to know more than some surface details for other smaller characters. In other words, if you have some bartender that pours a drink and says nothing then disappears... don't spend your energy writing a bio for them.

WHEN SHOULD YOU WRITE BIOS? >>>>>

After you've nailed down your story idea: genre, setting, subject, protagonist, antagonist, and the end, it's time to populate your story. You might have done some outlining of plot already, like an exploratory beat sheet of scenes and basic plot turns. *(It's a little more advanced to jump into outlines ahead of time. And we'll get into treatments later.)*

Sometime after you nailed down your story idea and around the time you lay out the basic plot... write the bios.

*Keep in mind, these bios will likely open up plot and story more than you know. Biographies can be extremely valuable tools to help you determine much of the plot, especially the protagonist's bio.

HOW DO YOU WRITE A BIOGRAPHY? >>>>>

The 100 questions included in the coming pages were created from a mix of intuition and design. Over the years, questions have been adjusted, added, and subtracted. None of the questions are insignificant. Although it might appear that one is at first, answer it anyway because:

This is a voyage of discovery!

*Some amazing jewels about your character may lurk in tiny and unusual places.

Some of the 100 questions include tips and guides, but most you'll already know how to handle. Some questions may only inspire a one-word answer; others may prompt you to write a paragraph. Write as much as you need to, but try to keep it to the question you're on and stay away from prose writing. We'll get to that later.

After these 100 questions, there's a little more road for you to travel with the bio. I'll meet you there…

DRAMATIC NEED >>>>>

In conjunction with your hero's dramatic want that you determined earlier, they should lack a few things they need. These needs are going to drive them, and the plot, forward.

INNER NEED

Inner need is a place of deficiency or immaturity in your hero that requires filling in order to attain the thing they want. It could be they lack courage, or the ability to trust, or simply a belief in themselves. Once you instill this lack in your hero, it will be up to you to design challenges to force them into choices that make them grow and resolve that need.

Inner needs using the character examples above:

- Frodo needs to trust his friends

- Luke Skywalker needs to believe in himself, and the force
- Elle needs to rely on her own intelligence
- Solomon needs to keep hope alive
- Wesley needs to believe in love again

OUTER NEEDS

Outer need is the single action the hero will need to take to overcome the forces of antagonism to claim their desire.

Outer needs using the examples above:

- Frodo needed to throw the one ring into Mt. Doom
- Luke Skywalker needs to learn the force, and how to fight
- Elle needed to get a Harvard law degree
- Solomon needed to play weak in order to survive
- Wesley needed to win his fortune and battle the evil prince

One of the most famous in movie history is the protagonist/hero Neo in 'The Matrix':

- **Outer need:** Learn to fight so he can challenge the Matrix.
- **Inner need:** to believe in himself beyond the physical. (His mentor, Morpheus, literally states, 'He's beginning to believe' during one pivotal story moment when Neo stops trying to physically fight the bad guys.)

That was a sign that Neo was ready to take on his biggest foe, and transform into the hero.

These needs are challenging writer choices to make because they will affect your entire story. So for now, use your intuition, and a little logic, and write down the protagonist's dramatic want, along with their inner and outer need in brief terms. Ultimately you could boil it down to as little as one word.

This bio creation process is going to be fluid. As you learn about your characters, you'll adjust things like needs and wants.

But once again it bears repeating:

Trust the process.

THE 100 QUESTIONS >>>>>

Dramatic Want: *State the #1 thing your character wants more than anything.*

For the protagonist, you should already know this from designing your story idea.

Now start answering these questions one-by-one until you get to 100. Think about people you know and borrow traits.

Have fun! Be imaginative. Go deep. Be fearless!

1. What is his/her mind like? *Is he/she sane or insane?*

2. What does he/she think about?

3. Does he/she recognize authority?

4. Does he/she have any pets?

5. What is his/her home like?

6. What gives him/her pleasure?

7. What kind of clothes does he/she wear?

8. Does he/she have friends or someone he/she confides in?

9. Relationship status?

10. Business partners?

11. How does he/she see himself?

12. How does he/she deal with conflict?

13. Did he/she ever join a team?

14. What does he/she dream about?

15. What does he/she think about his/her age?

16. What does he/she think about the future?

17. What does he/she want from the future?

18. What kind of friend is he/she?

19. What does he/she like about himself?

20. What does he/she dislike about himself?

21. Has he/she ever hurt someone?

22. Any unfulfilled ambitions?

23. Is he/she prejudice? Racist?

24. When does he/she like attention?

25. When would he/she be loud in public?

26. Does he/she admire anyone?

27. Does he/she have enemies?

28. What kind of humor does he/she have?

29. How does he/she laugh?

30. Is he/she practical or a dreamer?

31. Capable of intimacy?

32. Leader or follower?

33. Past emotional traumas?

34. Extrovert or introvert?

35. Ever seriously injured?

36. Where does he/she like to be touched?

37. Greatest success?

38. Greatest failure?

39. What are his/her talents?

40. Flaws?

41. Strengths?

42. Habits?

43. Manners?

44. Hangouts?

45. Best physical trait?

46. Worst physical trait?

47. What kind of diet does he/she have?

48. Favorite foods? Drinks?

49. Neat or sloppy?

50. Thorough or lackadaisical?

51. Secrets?

52. Weaknesses?

53. Favorite possessions?

54. Where is he/she most at home *(specifically)*?

55. Country or city; Elegant surroundings or rustic cabin?

56. How does he/she act in public?

57. What is his/her posture like?

58. Does he/she watch TV? What does he/she watch?

59. What does he/she read?

60. Does he/she read when he/she is taking a shit?

61. What sport does he/she like?

62. Does he/she take naps? For how long and where?

63. Does he/she like fast food?

64. Does he/she take drugs?

65. Has he/she ever traveled? Where?

66. What kind of car does he/she drive? Why?

67. Is there anything tangible he/she wants? Like an object.

68. Does he/she have a favorite color?

69. How much money does he/she make? And have?

70. What kind of underwear does he/she wear?

71. Does he/she have glasses?

72. What chores does he/she like?

73. What job does he/she hate?

74. Is there anyone he/she hates?

75. What is his/her favorite word?

76. What is his/her least favorite word?

77. What is his/her favorite curse word?

78. Does he/she exercise?

79. Does he/she carry a wallet? What's in it?

80. What is his/her favorite music?

81. What is his/her favorite vice?

Physical Description:

- Simple facts about body and appearance -

82. Sex? male or female

83. Age?

84. Height and weight?

85. Color of hair, eyes, skin?

86. Personal physical appearance? Good-looking, ugly, over or under weight, birth marks, diseases.

87. Heredity? Family traits. Alcoholism, longevity, etc.

Sociology:

- Their place in the world around them -

88. What social and economic class?

89. What is his/her occupation?

TIP: this can be very important, especially when deciding on his/her 'defining action'. (Described below)

90. Was or is he/she good in school?

91. Does he/she follow politics?

92. What where his/her parents like?

93. Does he/she believe in a god or follow religion?

94. Race, nationality? *White, black, Asian, etc: you can be as broad or specific as you want, narrowing to a region, country, or town. *This may also be story specific.*

Mindset:

This section bears description from you. It's less about single answers and it comes last because by now, you have probably learned a lot about your character to help you form his/her mindset.

95. What is his/her sex life like? *Desires, morality, physicality.*

96. Personal premise?

TIP: just like a story has a premise, your character will have a principle he/she lives by. His/her code.

97. Temperament?

TIP: this speaks to the way he/she deals with others. i.e. - choleric, easygoing, pessimistic, optimistic.

98. Attitude toward life?

TIP: this speaks to themes that govern his thinking. i.e. - Resigned, militant, defeatist, etc.

99. Complexes? *Obsessions, inhibitions, superstitions*. Exceptional abilities? *Imagination, judgment, taste, poise.*

100. His/her I.Q.?

WRITING IS REWRITING >>>>>

Put the questions and your answers away for a day or two before you look through them again. Then, come back and read your answers.

Expand on what you wrote if you find new things. Delete bits that don't seem to fit. Highlight areas of special importance. But most importantly:

Look for trends in your character.

You will probably see that he/she has a tendency toward being a certain way: angry, cruel, happy, peaceful. Trends are good things to note, but be careful that you haven't created a one-dimensional character, or a cliché.

All characters have goods and bads, ups and downs, even conflicting ways inside of them. Have you found these conflicts in your character? If not, can you create some?

A reminder from the chapter, "CAPTURE AND MAGNIFY YOUR STORY IDEA":

Conflict is King!

Go through the bios a couple of times to expand and highlight. Remember you're shaping them to fit your story. Polarize them, force them into corners, design the flaws. You're preparing them to take a journey, face problems, to be great or to be weak.

*Try to create each bio one at a time before moving to the next character. Take about a day for each pass. If plot ideas pop in your head while learning your characters, jot those down in a separate place and use them when you design your structure.

SUMMARY >>>>>

These last points are a culmination of what you have learned about your character and will link to the plot structure via the **defining action**.

**Use these last 5 points as a short reference guide to your character as you're writing your story.*

1. Dramatic want = *restate the #1 thing your character wants more than anything. (Has is changed or clarified?)*

2. Point of View = *TIP: you can mine questions 96, 97, and 98 to help with this. Point of view is how the character sees their place in the world. And by way of that, how they see the world itself as it relates to them.*

3. Attitude = *TIP: You've already answered this in question 98, but you can expand on it here.*

4. Change = *TIP: By the end of your story, does your character change from what he/she was at the beginning?*

5. Defining action = *TIP: create an action that this character will be doing when we first meet them in your story. The action should be indicative of who they are and what they are about. It could be* *his/her job, or an activity that they love. (**Introduce each character through a defining action)*

Example of a defining action: (ROCKY) Rocky was first introduced in a crappy gym where he was fighting an unfair boxing match where the fans utterly disrespected him.

FINAL EXERCISE >>>>>

Now that you have all this great information about your character, you can use it to write as long of a history as you want about them.

This is where you can expand in prose form and let yourself 'feel' for them. Infuse emotion into them from how you feel. Let them speak if they want. Tell how they feel, or felt, about a situation that happened in their history.

Design their bios right up to
the moment your story begins.

Once finished, you should have a long document, could be 10 pages or more for each character, detailing everything. It should include the following four sections:

1. Stated dramatic wants and needs
2. The answered and highlighted 100 questions
3. The 5 summary questions
4. A prose-like recap of your character's history and traits.

"**YOU'RE NEVER GOING TO KILL STORYTELLING** BECAUSE IT'S BUILT INTO THE HUMAN PLAN."

- MARGARET ATWOOD

A HANDMAID'S TALE

CHAPTER 5
STRUCTURE AT A GLANCE

STRUCTURE: YOU MAY NOT LIKE IT NOW, BUT YOU'LL LOVE IT LATER! >>>>>

THIS CHAPTER IS A STRAIGHTFORWARD DIVE into story structure. It gives you an overview of the three-act structure concept, as well as supplying you with all the elements needed to build a solid plot outline. It's meant to be interactive, like the rest of this book. So hold on to your hat...

When you finish, you'll have all the major and most minor plot points, the sequence themes governing each section of a three-act structure, and a firm grasp of how your protagonist drives, and is subject to, the plot's structure.

Make no mistake, **structure is form,** and it seems that the first thing most writer's want to do is buck conformity. You're artists after all, of course you'll fight the norm!

Outlines, structures, frameworks; seems like they're meant to confine you, but learning how they work, and work for you, will set the stage for your creativity to be unleashed. You did it already by building a box around your idea. But if that doesn't convince you, maybe take the word of one of history's greatest rule-breaking artists:

'Learn the rules like a pro,
so you can break them like an artist.'
~ Pablo Picasso

Picasso himself painted traditional-style portraits before he went down the road of abstraction and broke the mould forever.

Knowing the rules and how to play with them will help you hook an audience, and keep them with you, even in the most 'outside the lines' plot you can dream up. It's because there are expectations, well known to story-loving audiences, that you can accentuate, or use as hooks to draw people into new ground. If you don't know them, how can you use them?

Following THE SCREENWRITER'S WAY process from the start, you should have created tons of material to work with already:

> Genre, Setting, Subject, Protagonist, Antagonist, and your Ending. You should also be prepared with a pile of character biographies for your cast.

With those elements in mind and at the ready, because you'll need them to build your plot, let's add one more piece of framework to your budding story: ***timeframe***.

TIMEFRAME >>>>>

This was mentioned in the ideas chapter while you were defining your setting.

Timeframe defines the amount of time
that passes during the telling of your story from
FADE IN to FADE OUT,
or
Once upon a time... and The End.

Does your story take place over a week or a year or a day or a life-time? Here are a few examples of timeframe to get you thinking:

'Forest Gump' - about 4-decades
'American Beauty' - a couple of months
'Before Sunrise' - a few hours over a single night
'Dog Day Afternoon' - real time (movie run time was the character's timeframe too - 125 minutes.)

You can see in those stories how timeframe dramatically changes every aspect of the story from themes to locations to character development and more. Those timeframes were also designed to allow for character change (arc) and force subject-specific conflict.

It's a good rule of thumb to consider that short timeframes often elicit intimate character stories because you have to go into minute detail in order to fill your pages. While longer time periods aid in telling large thematic pieces.

Now is the time to determine the passage of time in your story. Use your own life when thinking about the timeframe. What has happened to you in certain periods? How much time do your characters need in order to arc, and change? Are there physical considerations, like a historical event that has to unfold? Or what about a character growing up and getting old?

Write down your timeframe now.

STRUCTURE BASICS >>>>>

In the chapter, 'Capture and Magnify Your Story Idea' it showed that creativity happens INSIDE the box. It's a container to focus your idea and demand creativity.

Story structure is another form of a creative box:

Framework defined by acts,
plot points, sequences and scenes.

In keeping with earlier themes, it might be helpful to think of your plot structure like the map guiding you on the journey. Intuition formed your compass, boxing up your story idea was like identifying your North Star. You built a cast of companions with character bios. The plot map is the path your hero takes, but it's also the map guiding you in the writing. It's as if you and your hero are taking the same journey!

Movies and screenplays work in a three-act structure that began with the Greeks and Aristotle. Most movies use it and audiences know it well.

Let's build your understanding of plot structure slowly. Take your time with this, I'm going to repeat and expand each piece as we move through the chapter until you have the full picture.

Trust the process!

Three-Act structure is as simple as:

1.) beginning
2.) middle
3.) end.

Or, a person, does something, and there's a result.

Act 1: Set Up *(a person)*
Act 2: Conflict *(does something)*
Act 3: Resolution *(result)*

We're aiming at a screenplay that runs about 110 pages **(That's 1 script page per minute of movie run time.)** Your total page count divides, per act, approximately like this:

- Act 1, the Set Up, is about 30 pages
- Act 2, the Conflict, is about 60 pages
- Act 3, the Resolution, is about 20 pages

Those page counts are not set in stone, but pretty close. You can miss your target page count by a few pages and still be okay. If your total screenplay page count is higher than 110, adjust the page counts proportionally in each Act, but try to keep Act 1 as close to 30 pages as possible.

PLOT POINTS >>>>>

So that you know where you're aiming, here is a simple breakdown of the structural plot points you're going to create for your story:

- PAGE 1 or close to it: Inciting Incident – something happens that will change your hero's world forever.
- PAGE 5: Statement of theme – overarching theme you're going to prove in your story.
- PAGE 12: Stimulus – something personal about the inciting incident lands in the hero's path.
- PAGE 17: Foreshadow end of Act 1 by challenging the hero with a problem or offering something they want.
- PAGE 30: Plot Point 1 – **End of Act 1** the hero makes an irrevocable action-oriented choice to take up the cause.
- PAGE 45: False Hope – The hero's regular bag of tricks looks like it's working to help him achieve success. *It's a False Hope, because in the next moment you find out that his game isn't working and he's going to have to change tactics.*
- PAGE 60: **Midpoint** – the hero goes from passive to active in the pursuit of his/her destiny.
- PAGE 75: False Ending – after changing tactics and beating some antagonists, the hero looks like they have won the day. *Like the False Epiphany, the 'False Ending'*

proves that the 'win' was not real in the next moment, because things go very much awry.

- PAGE 90: ROCK BOTTOM – **End of Act 2 -** Everything that could go wrong for the hero has gone wrong, and they look like they are doomed.
- PAGE 100: Choice to rally and pursue the prize.

Plot points define act and sequence breaks. They also represent moments when your protagonist makes significant choices that define his/her character as he/she pursues their want.

Major Plot Points:

~ Page 30 : Plot Point 1 – protagonist irrevocably chooses to pursue his/her goal. End of Act 1

~ Page 60 : Midpoint – protagonist makes a choice that takes him/her from passive to active in the pursuit of his/her destiny.

~ Page 90 : Plot point 2 - Rock Bottom – protagonist loses everything and is as far from his/her goal as possible. This happens at the end of Act 2.

Minor Plot Points:

~ By page 5 (but as close to page 1 as possible) : Inciting Incident, light the fuse.

~ Page 12 : Stimulus - set up page 17 moment.

~ Page 17 : Call to adventure - foreshadow Plot Point 1. Introduce the central question.

~ Page 45 : False hope – protagonist thinks his/her passive actions are winning.

~ Page 75 : False ending – protagonist thinks he/she has won. Seems like a happy ending could happen here.

~ Page 100 : Climax begins - Protagonist chooses to return from exile (loss) with a new hope, and challenge their nemesis for the prize.

ACT AND SEQUENCE THEMES >>>>>

Acts 1, 2, and 3 each have story-specific themes that define them. They break into sub-themes that define sequences within each act.

The sequences have mini-themes that define the kinds of scenes that occur within them and will help you choose actions and design scenes and even dialogue.

Here's a basic rundown of the generic act and sequence themes that you will make specific later:

Act 1: Pages 1-30 = The Set Up

> Pages 1-10: Introductions

> Pages 11-20: Expand protagonist and set up problem

> Pages 21-30: Refusal of the call

Act 2: Pages 30-90 = Conflict

The second act is a little bit more complex than Act 1.

First, you will identify the overarching Act 2 conflict specific to *your* story and protagonist's goal.

Example:
Overall Act 2 theme of 'The Matrix' =
Neo wants to destroy the matrix.
(This falls under the generic Act 2 theme of conflict.)

Next, Act 2 has a first and second half divided by a central pillar in your structure called the **Midpoint**. It's significant because events and characters will dramatically change after the midpoint. The hero will go from passive to active in the pursuit of their want.

Each of the two halves of Act 2 carries a sub-theme that grows from the overall Act 2 theme. Those are divided again into sequences with themes.

Here are the generic themes:

> Act 2: Part 1: Pages 30-60 = Passive actions

>> Sequence 1, Pages 30-45 = Reaction to new world

>> Sequence 2, Pages 46-60 = Begin to transform, old ways die

> Act 2: Part 2: Pages 60-90 = Dynamic actions

>> Sequence 3, Pages 60-75 = Bad guys close in

>> Sequence 4, Pages 76-90 = Efforts thwarted

Example:

Act 2: Part 1 theme of 'The Matrix' =

Neo trains/prepares to fight in the matrix.

But as he enters Act 2: Part 2, his actions become dynamic and the theme reflects that.

At the Act 2 Midpoint, the theme shifts as Neo enters the matrix to fight.

Act 3: Pages 90-110: Resolution

> Pages 90-100 = Defeat and wallow in misery

> Pages 100-110 = Return from exile, new hope (climax begins)

After your hero captures the prize (his/her want) and all plot and subplots are resolved, which they should be by this point, you end on the emotional high point and FADE OUT.

Each of the sequence defining themes helps guide you while designing the kinds of scenes you need to create, how those scenes progress, and how characters will react. **Imagine what kinds of scenes happens during Neo trains, then when he fights.*

Now that you have a birds-eye view of each Act: their defining plot points, and the generic Act and sequence themes… your head is probably spinning. Don't worry, we're going to go over them in more detail in a minute.

What's your mantra? ***Trust the process…***

So, take heart… and take a look at the diagram included on the next page to help you visualize Acts, plot points, and act sequences as one map that puts it all together. Then we'll get more detailed in the following pages.

Study the diagram for a minute and get familiar with it, because soon you're going to make your own. Try to imagine it like a map of you and your hero's journey.

**There is also a larger version of this structure diagram in the appendix at the back of this book.*

PLOT STRUCTURE DIAGRAM >>>>>

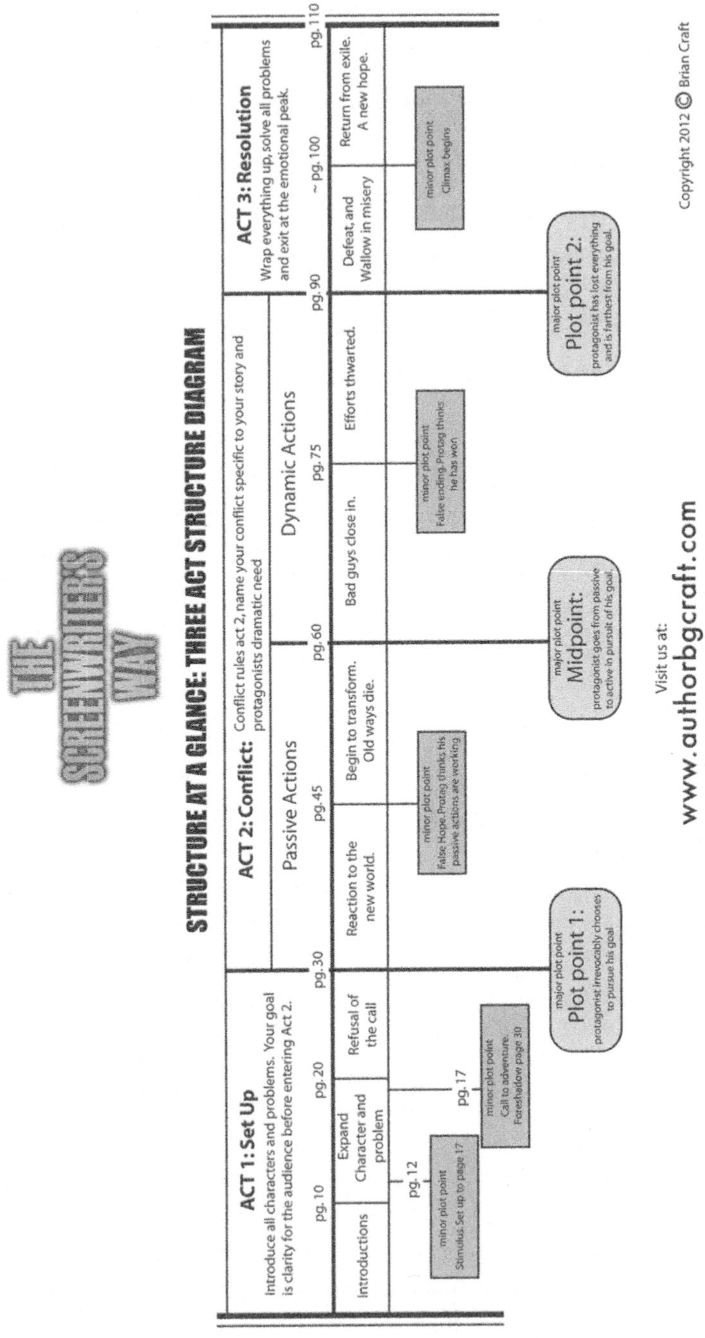
THE SCREENWRITER'S WAY
STRUCTURE AT A GLANCE: THREE ACT STRUCTURE DIAGRAM
ACT 1: Set Up
Introduce all characters and problems. Your goal is clarity for the audience before entering Act 2.
ACT 2: Conflict: Conflict rules act 2, name your conflict specific to your story and protagonists dramatic need
Passive Actions
Dynamic Actions
ACT 3: Resolution
Wrap everything up, solve all problems and exit at the emotional peak.
pg. 10
pg. 20
pg. 30
pg. 45
pg. 60
pg. 75
pg. 90
~ pg. 100
pg. 110
Introductions
Expand Character and problem
Refusal of the call
Reaction to the new world.
Begin to transform. Old ways die.
Bad guys close in.
Efforts thwarted.
Defeat, and Wallow in misery
Return from exile. A new hope.
pg. 12
minor plot point Stimulus: Set up to page 17
pg. 17
minor plot point Call to adventure. Foreshadow page 30
major plot point Plot point 1: protagonist irrevocably chooses to pursue his goal
minor plot point False Hope. Protag thinks his passive actions are working
major plot point Midpoint: protagonist goes from passive to active in pursuit of his goal.
minor plot point False ending. Protag thinks he has won
major plot point Plot point 2: protagonist has lost everything and is farthest from his goal.
minor plot point Climax begins.
Visit us at:
www.authorbgcraft.com
Copyright 2012 © Brian Craft

TENTPOLES IN YOUR STRUCTURE >>>>>

Now let's expand these ideas and start building your story structure. This is where you will begin to define, specifically, how each theme and plot point will shape *your* story.

Let's ramp up to making plot-structure choices with a powerful reminder:

***The protagonist drives everything in your story.**

Knowing his/her #1 dramatic want drives the nature of your structure choices. (You should have decided this while writing the protagonist's bio.)

Ready?

Let's make your first 'tentpole' structure choices:

Step 1. State your ending. You should already know it from defining your story idea.

Step 2. Define **Plot Point 2**; it's at the end of Act 2 at page 90. At this point in your story the protagonist has lost EVERYTHING in the pursuit of his/her want. *He/she is at rock bottom.* (To help you: decide everything that he/she lost.)

Step 3. Define **Plot Point 1**; it's at the end of Act 1 at page 30. The protagonist faces a choice that will lead him/her to their goal; he must *choose his path and then take action* to step over a threshold into the conflict of Act 2. *This is a point of no return. Your hero's choice is irrevocable, forcing them into conflict, and transformation.*

Step 4. Decide where the story begins. The opening page should be interesting enough to grab us immediately. It sets tone, expresses genre and setting, starts the clock ticking on your time-frame, and may include the inciting incident.

Step 5. Design the **Inciting Incident** - an event that will change the protagonist's life forever. *For example:*

> ***'AVATAR':*** *Jake Sully arrives at Pandora (theatrical version.)*
> ***'DUMB AND DUMBER'****: Lloyd meets Mary Swanson.*
> ***'STAR WARS'****: C3-PO and R2D2 eject to Luke's planet carrying secret plans for the Death Star.*

Step 6. Determine the **Midpoint** of Act 2. (It's also the midpoint of your story.) **This is the moment your protagonist makes a *choice* to move from passive to active in the pursuit of his destiny (want or goal).**

Use the structure diagram to help you visualize. **I highly recommend you take out a piece of paper, draw the framework of the structure diagram, and fill in your own plot points and themes.

STRUCTURE AT A GLANCE >>>>>

With your structure tentpoles in place, let's dive deeper. The best way to learn is to do! Trial by fire. You're going to create, erase, recreate, and think about these plot points and themes over and over until you get them exactly how you want them.

Take your time with this, and don't get frustrated, this part is challenging. But it's also fun, because every challenge, and each hole, is an opportunity to explore and create!

ACT 1: THE SET UP

ACT 1 introduces the protagonist and his/her dramatic want, all the other major and supporting characters, the stakes, and the genre. Your goal here is clarity; you want your audience to completely understand the rules of your world and the fight your hero is about to engage.

The audience must know what this story is about, with no doubt or confusion, before your hero crosses Plot Point 1 and enters Act 2.

Sequential Theme for Pages 1-10:

- **Introductions**: Introduce the protagonist, his/her problem, and the inciting incident. State the theme. You're introducing the elements of your story.

Plot Points for Pages 1-10:

- **Opening page** - grab the audience immediately! Might be exciting, but definitely interesting. Might include the inciting incident. **You already decided some of this with your tentpoles.*

- **Inciting Incident** – before page 10, but ideally as close as possible to page 1. A major kick off event that will change the hero's world forever. Whether the protagonist is present or not, it should impact him/her. *This lights the fuse of your story. *There are examples at the end of this chapter to help you.*

- **Page 5: Statement of theme** - The protagonist will likely encounter a minor character that will state the overall story theme. This is something you, as the writer, are going to prove by telling this story. *i.e. – Face your demons to be free.*

**Although not listed as such, this is important and might be considered a minor plot point. However, you often discover the story theme through writing your first draft, so you may choose to wait on this point and develop it later.

Sequential Theme for Pages 11-20:

- **Expand Character and Set up problem**: Expand on the protagonist's life. (Who he is, where does he live, what's his job? etc.) Within this section, you will also introduce the stimulus at page 12, and present your hero with a choice at page 17. (Pages 12 and 17 contain minor plot points.)

Plot Points for Pages 11-20:

- **Page 12 – a stimulus** that emphasizes the inciting incident and sets up the page 17 moment. *For example: Someone is in trouble and needs help. Maybe a bank got robbed… and the hero is stimulated into action because her life-savings was robbed too (she WANTS to buy a home with it.)*

This is also a good place to introduce possible love interest. If you have a love interest, they often form a substantial subplot that helps expose the inner motives of your hero/protagonist.

- **Page 17 – call to adventure.** Foreshadow the Act 1 plot point at upcoming page 30. This is a moment when the page 30 choice enters the protagonist's world. i.e. *-The hero is asked for help by the troubled person. Or maybe she's an ex-FBI agent with a special skill and her boss asks her to help track the thieves that robbed the bank, and her money.*

This also introduces the central question of your story. i.e. - *Will he/she succeed and save the person, retrieve the money, win the prize?* <<< You must answer this before your story ends.

Sequential Theme for Pages 21-30:

- **Refusal of the Call:** soon after page 17, the protagonist may be unconvinced to take action. He/she may seek out or get introduced to their mentor, look for more information about the problem they face, be engaged by the antagonist, or otherwise be pressed to make a choice.

Plot Points for Pages 21-30:

- **Page 28 – Visit with the mentor:** This isn't a plot point as such, but it's a good springboard to include. This is where the hero visits their mentor to get a final piece of information before making their big choice.

- **Page 30: Plot Point 1 – protagonist makes a choice that ends Act 1**. This is the point of no return that launches him into the conflict of Act 2.

**30 is a major plot point (Plot Point 1); It needs to be clear and should be defined through an action. It moves the protagonist from the *ordinary world* into the *special world* of your story's Act 2. When that happens, everything should reflect that change from setting, to people, to philosophy, etc.

For example: 'The Matrix': Neo meets Morpheus and chooses to take the red pill (symbolic threshold). Then he physically walks over the threshold into the next room (literal threshold). After a little techo-stuff, Neo wakes up in an entirely new reality.

Summing up what happens in Act 1: Some event (Inciting Incident) occurs in your hero's world that will change everything. By page 12 (stimulus), that Inciting Incident connects to your hero personally and sets up a moment that happens on page 17 (foreshadow of your page 30 Plot Point 1). Page 17 engages the hero directly. They might be asked to join a fight, they might see that a fight is coming, they might receive an offer to join an expedition, or maybe they find out exactly where their romantic interest will be. From pages 17 to nearly page 30, the hero will resist this 'call to adventure'. But by page 30, events will keep pushing the hero toward making a choice to pursue the prize. He/she will make an action-defined choice to cross a threshold into Act 2 and enter conflict. The step into Act 2 is irrevocable. He/she might blast off in a ship to Mars, or take action on a case to solve a crime. Anything that is a step they can't take back.

What are these things in your hero's world?

Set-up is insanely important. Almost all story problems can be traced back to a poorly designed set up. So take your time, work this over and over before continuing your journey.

ACT 2: CONFLICT – Part 1: Passive Action: Pages 30-60

In many ways, ACT 2 displays a transformation of the protagonist and we must motivate this change through the change in themes.

In Act 2, the hero fully engages the antagonist in pursuit of his/her goal. Thus, the overarching theme of Act 2 is 'Conflict'. But you must define the specific nature of *your* story's conflict. *For example: 'Neo wants to destroy the matrix'*. Once you know that, you will split it into 2 parts separated by the Midpoint.

Passive actions will govern the conflict in Act 2 Part 1: Pages 30-60. *For example: The Matrix: Neo trains to fight, learns about the matrix.*

Sequential Theme Pages 31-45:

- **Reaction**: Protagonist reacts to the new path he/she is on and the problem he has engaged, but in a passive way. He also gathers allies and information. In other words, the hero thinks he can get what he wants by doing things the way he always has. *That mindset leads to page 45 minor plot point; the false hope.*

Plot Points for Pages 31-45:

- Page 45 – False hope – The passive actions of the protagonist make him believe his pursuit is going well.

Directly following page 45, the hope is dashed and a new problem is presented that will likely be resolved at page 75.

Sequential Theme Pages 46-60:

- **Begin to transform. Old ways die:** many of the helpful forces and the protagonist's old ways of gaining success strip away. He may become isolated, lose his love interest (temporarily), or have a disagreement with the mentor. But the path he's on has taught him something new that he'll engage at the midpoint.

Plot Points for Pages 46-60:

- Page 46, or close to 46, is a soft, minor plot point that acts like a companion to Page 45 and emphasizes, 'False hope', by doing something negative to show that the satisfaction the hero experienced at 45 was, in fact, false.

- Page 60 – Midpoint – Protagonist takes decisive action to engage his/her problem on his/her own terms, both internally and externally.

Midpoint is also a major plot point and one of the most important moments in the story. It truly defines the protagonist/hero because it cements his transformation as he take action of his own toward his destiny.

Summing up what happens in the first part of Act 2: The hero/protagonist made a choice that dropped them into a whole new reality; the 'special world' of Act 2. The people look and act different, the setting changes dramatically, and the hero must find allies and information. They do things the way they have always done it, and they have fun doing it. They seem well on their way to winning and even might get a taste of victory at page 45 (the false hope). But then they meet disappointment almost immediately and find out that they weren't doing as good as they thought... the victory slips away. Now they need to challenge their old ways and really start to use their newfound skills of navigating the 'special world'. They shift tactics but are still passive in their pursuit. That comes in the form of reactionary choices to events and sources of antagonism. The hero over-extends and finds themselves bumping into the midpoint (page 60). This is a culture shock moment. Either they get themself together and take action, or the antagonist is going to run away with the prize.

ACT 2: CONFLICT – Part 2: Dynamic Action: Pages 61-90

The overarching theme of Act 2 is 'Conflict'. Remember to define the specific nature of the conflict in *your* story.

Dynamic actions will govern the conflict in Act 2 Part 2: Pages 61-90. *For example: The Matrix: Neo enters the matrix to fight.*

Sequential Theme Pages 61-75:

- **Bad guys close in**: As the hero takes action, he/she is exposed to more danger and antagonistic forces surround him. But he/she escapes this problem by 75.

Plot Points for Pages 61-75:

- Page 75 – False ending – The dynamic actions of the protagonist make them believe that at this point they have achieved their goal. He/she might even have it in hand. **If you stopped the story/movie right here it would seem like a happy ending.*

Directly following page 75, the protagonist realizes they don't have their goal, or it is taken away from them. Things will get worse.

Sequential Theme Pages 76-90:

- **Efforts thwarted:** Ramp down to 'rock bottom': Protagonist's actions are defeated and everything is taken from him/her. His/her journey is in danger of failure.

Plot Point Pages 76-90:

- Page 76, or close to 76, is a soft, minor plot point that acts like a companion to Page 75 and emphasizes, 'False ending', by doing something negative to show that the joy the hero experienced at 75 was, in fact, false.

- Page 90 – Rock Bottom – Protagonist arrives at a point where EVERYTHING has gone wrong. He/she is as far away from success as is possible and has no one, and nothing, to help them.

*Protagonist is now the furthest away from the page 17 goal.

One of the best examples of 'rock bottom' is 'The Shawshank Redemption'. Protagonist, Andy Dufresne, finds out that he will never get out of prison, and that his efforts to 'game' the system at the prison are the very things that dictate his failure. Also, his efforts in prison turned him from being a truly innocent man into a criminal by helping the warden. To define his failure through action, he is thrown in solitary confinement for two months.

The central question at page 17 of 'The Shawshank Redemption' is "Will Andy stay sane and get out of prison?" At page 90 he is as far from that as possible.

Summing up what happens in the second part of Act 2: The hero made another major decision at the Midpoint to actively pursue his/her want. They are making choices that are no longer passive or reactionary. At that moment, the bad guys (sources of antagonism) are actively fighting the hero. It looks like the hero is winning, and at page 75 seems like he/she did! Until moments later when victory is snatched away and things begin to unravel. Friends and allies may be taken out of the picture, the hero's efforts start to wobble, and they come to a crashing halt at page 90, Rock Bottom. Now they are not only losing, but they are in a worse position than before they started this journey to begin with.

He/she can't go home, and they can't stay here!

ACT 3: RESOLUTION: Pages 90-110?

ACT 3 resolves your story. It reflects Act 1 in many ways because it returns the protagonist to his 'ordinary world', and takes him/her to a place where he/she will answer the central question, and win or lose the goal set up in Act 1.

The ending should feel both inevitable and surprising. Inevitable because we have taken the journey with our intrepid hero; we believe in them, and we know they can do it. But surprising because you, as the writer, should keep the prize out of arms reach until the very last moment.

Sequential Theme Pages 91-100:

- **Defeat and wallow in misery**: The protagonist saw utter defeat at the end of Act 2. He/she will flounder, or stumble through a couple of scenes until they realize that they must accept their transformation. He/she must bring their newfound knowledge, gained through their journey, back to the ordinary world and engage the antagonist in a final fight for all the stakes.

Plot Point for Pages 91-The End:

- Page 100 – Protagonist makes a final decision to go for the prize with his newfound knowledge. At this point, he/she is often visited by a mentor, or another minor character (a goddess, or feminine energy according to Joseph Campbell. Because she is appealing to the hero's inner needs and encouraging him/her to believe in themselves) that prompts the hero-to-be into taking action.

Sequential Theme Pages 100-110:

- **Climax and end:** this is less a theme, and more of a directive to wrap everything up. By now, you probably know exactly what the protagonist should do, because you already stated the ending when we started the process of our writer's journey together.

The start of this sequence is often emphasized with a scene of the protagonist running, or taking a short, fast journey of some kind *(You'll see this in every movie now that you know about it. Tom Cruise seems to have mastered it.)* It designates the abandoning of the old ways and the embracing of the new.

*Heightening emotion is your major goal for Act 3. Increase the intensity until you reach the climax at its emotional peak and then END YOUR STORY.

For example: STAR WARS: Luke is in a pitched space battle where he's really showing his fighter pilot skills. But then, when the rebels are in danger of losing it all, he embraces the force in a nearly impossible moment in order to destroy the Death Star. Once it explodes, there are a few, very brief, scenes to emphasize their victory and unity, and then BAM! the story ends in triumphant music. The audience leaves on a high. (And George Lucas kicked off the most successful franchise in movie history.)

All issues, questions, and story lines must be resolved by the time you FADE OUT. Be clear, decisive and express conviction about your story's ending.

ONE FINAL STORY NOTE >>>>>

*A protagonist IS NOT a hero while they are on their journey, **the journey transforms them into a hero.** But this is only validated at the very end, when they take action as their newly transformed self to defeat their antagonist. They aren't a hero before that specific action. Usually, this involves them completing an inner journey that overcomes their flaws. They become courageous, or loving, or trusting and that becomes the key to victory.

I guarantee you that Luke blowing up the Death Star would have been spectacular, but not emotionally satisfying if he hadn't believed in himself and used the force (because that lets ME and YOU believe in our own ability to overcome, too!)

Make your hero earn it in every single way possible!

PLOT POINT EXAMPLES >>>>>

- Inciting Incident

WEDDING CRASHERS – new wedding crashing season is open.

AMERICAN BEAUTY – Lester's boss informs him he must write a letter to save himself from being fired.

THE MATRIX – Neo is contacted by Morpheus about The Matrix.

- Page 17, Foreshadow end of Act 1

WEDDING CRASHERS – John first sees Claire.

AMERICAN BEAUTY – Lester meets Angela and is smitten – he has his first fantasy about her.

THE MATRIX – Neo tries to escape the agents with Morpheus' help.

- Page 30, Plot Point 1: End of Act 1

WEDDING CRASHERS - John accepts invitation to the Cleary's (Claire's) home for the weekend.

AMERICAN BEAUTY – Lester joins Ricky to get high.

THE MATRIX – Neo chooses to take the red pill and learn what the Matrix is.

- Page 45, False hope

WEDDING CRASHERS - John asks to join Claire for a night walk.

AMERICAN BEAUTY – Lester confronts Caroline about sex after she catches him masturbating.

THE MATRIX – Neo learns he is the key to destroying the Matrix.

- Page 60, Midpoint

WEDDING CRASHERS - John admits he's falling for Claire and gets help from Jeremy to catch her.

AMERICAN BEAUTY – Lester blackmails his boss for money after delivering a scathing letter.

THE MATRIX – Neo asks if he will be able to dodge bullets. (He wants to fight.)

- Page 75, False Epiphany

WEDDING CRASHERS – John spends the day with Claire, they kiss on the beach.

AMERICAN BEAUTY – Lester and Caroline almost make amends as Lester comes on to her sexually.

THE MATRIX – Neo reenters the Matrix and his old life.

- Page 90, Plot point 2: End of Act 2, Rock Bottom

WEDDING CRASHERS - John and Jeremy are found out, Claire hates him, they are ejected from the Cleary's home.

AMERICAN BEAUTY – Lester catches Caroline and Buddy cheating on him while he works at the burger joint.

THE MATRIX – Neo's team dies, antagonist captures Morpheus, and Neo ISN'T 'the one'.

FINAL EXERCISE >>>>>

Pick out movies similar to what you want to write or movies that are simply great, maybe Academy Award winners; sit down and watch them with pen and paper, or your story journal, or computer, at hand.

As you watch, write down each scene number, the nature of that scene and what happens (be brief), and the time the scene ends.

Pay attention to major plot points and sequence themes. Your goal is to understand how other stories work.

Example:

'Manhattan': by Woody Allen

Scene beats and thematic elements:

ACT 1

1. Open on images of Manhattan. V.O. of Isaac trying to write about the city he loves. It displays the differing points of view about New York. Opening introduces us to Isaac and the fact that

he is a TV writer in a crappy job; he's had several marriages and is dating a girl that is only 17 to his 42. Isaac is indecisive. This is the many stories and points of view of the city, and the fact that Isaac can't commit to one.

00.04.00 <<< *(ending time of the scene: **hours.minutes.seconds**)*

2. Enter a jazz club. Isaac gets drunk and talks about his life. A girl he's dating is less than half his age, his 2nd ex-wife is writing a book about their break up. << He's unlucky at love. It's exposition to show us that Isaac is bad at relationships. And can't spot a good thing when he sees it, i.e. his present girlfriend.

00.06.30

3. Inciting incident. - Yale and Isaac walk home. Yale confesses that he is having an affair. Introduces a problem, or maybe an opportunity = you can cheat! Instead of being with just one person romantically, you can have one and then try another. His married friend makes dating around okay by his admission.

00.08.30

SUMMARY >>>>>

Now you should have a list of your major and minor plot points, and the sequential and act themes that hold them together. Preferably in a chart form like earlier in this chapter so you can visually reference it quickly.

Doing all this work prior to creating scenes for your treatment will clarify your vision and make the process of screenwriting much more fun. It will also elevate the quality of your screenplay and set you apart from other writers.

Keep in mind that your structure is flexible and alive. As you learn more about your story while writing, you will adjust and clarify. Trust the process, it will set you free.

With your structure in hand, you're ready to invent scenes and write a treatment that will begin to infuse the emotion you have for your story and characters.

"THE GREAT THING ABOUT CINEMA AND FICTION IS THAT **ANYTHING YOU COME UP WITH CAN BECOME REAL.**"

- GEORGE LUCAS

THX 1138
AMERICAN GRAFFITI
STAR WARS
INDIANA JONES
INDUSTRIAL LIGHT AND MAGIC

CHAPTER 6
ENERGIZED TREATMENTS

"IT'S ALIVE! ALIVE!!" exclaimed Dr. Frankenstein when his monster finally animated and came to life. *(He was pretty excited.)* But only moments before, his creation lay still, a lifeless collection of sewn together body parts strapped to a surgical table. If you remember that legendary movie scene (based on the book), with the odd-but-brilliant scientific machines sparking wildly as a massive electrical storm raged outside the ancient gothic castle, you might also recall the feeling of terror and anticipation fueling the moment.

Bookmark that in your mind for a second...

Assuming you've nailed down genre, setting, subject and you created character bio's and a detailed plot structure: you now have a collection of shaped pieces and parts, assembled and strapped to your writing desk awaiting animation. Those are the raw materials of your story, but not the story just yet.

'Energized Treatments' refers to the need to inject energy into your story, animating it by infusing emotion.

Energize:

To give vitality and enthusiasm; to animate.

The treatment strategy detailed in this chapter prepares your story for scripting with vitality and enthusiasm. Ready to walk and talk just like Frankenstein's monster. There are different treatments or synopses that exist for pitching to producers, but for now it's about the writer's creative process.

That process is the same whether you're writing comedy, romance, horror, or any other genre. Our goal is 8-12 pages of prose-like writing, that encompasses your entire story, by describing each scene one-by-one. It should include emotion, intention, action and can even include bits of spontaneous dialogue.

This treatment is your story in as illustrated a way as you can imagine. It's akin to a fully colored and texturized version of your plot/structure map. But it also functions like a work order document for your screenplay since it includes scene numbers, expected run-time for each scene (which coincides with page count: 1-page per minute), and embeds your plot structure into it with call-outs marking where major points and act breaks occur.

When finished, this is going to be your bible when you sit down to write your script.

Emotion is the true product of a story or movie. It's what empty-handed audiences take away with them, and happily pay a premium to get. As artists we want to generate an equal or greater emotional reaction in an audience than we had at our moment of inspiration to write it.

Now that you've done most of the objective planning for your story, it's time to loosen up your imagination and revisit the vision that launched you on the writing journey in the first place.

The feelings and ideas you had when first inspired need to rise up again. Find clues in your creative research image file if you need a primer. Add to that file, shuffle things around. Refine your vision. Because unlike your first spark of inspiration, you have constraints now, which you created. Armed with your plot structure to guide you, it should keep you focused and help shape your creative choices.

Treatments are a sort of bridge in your screenwriting/storytelling process that links artistic expression and the functional realities of a script. Your story needs flavor, color, lingo, themes and metaphors that bring to life the human experience. It also needs function: like production references and adherence to screenplay format that shapes the telling. Things like the simple expression of a slug line with INT. or EXT. (Interior or Exterior), location call outs, and time of day for the scene.

Screenwriting is a craft,
your art thrives within its boundaries.

Your treatment will be robust with character's emotions, intentions and even some psychology that you realize about your characters. It might include little notes about relationships in the scenes (character to character, character to environment, or character to moment or plot), or maybe special props you want emphasize. It's like making notes to yourself about how you're going to shape things when you write the script itself.

And when you take this treatment into scripting, you'll be like a chef boiling down ingredients, reducing elements together to maximize flavor until even single droplets are taste explosions. In the process of writing the screenplay, you will turn **intentions into dialogue, express emotions as action,** and **turn psychology into character choices**.

***Let me say that again. When writing your script:*

- *Character intentions become dialogue.*
- *Emotions get expressed as actions.*
- *Psychology is illustrated through character choices.*

LOGLINES >>>>>

Quite often while writing a story you will 'zoom in and zoom out' of the landscape of your work. That means you'll get hyper-close to moments while deciding dialogue or designing a plot point, but then need to pull back and get a read on the story as a whole to see how things are lining up. *You'll do this constantly.*

In order to keep your story's goal in sight, and keep from getting dizzy as you zoom in and out while concepting scenes for your treatment, you need a North Star in the form of a clear, concise, and compelling **logline**:

One sentence, approximately 25-35 words in length, that describes your entire story.

It can be freakishly challenging to distill your story into one sentence and still make it compelling. It's a good test of your vision, and a first challenge of bridging art and craft.

**Here's a good trick to use when writing a logline: pretend you're telling a 5-year old child what your story is about.*

The Anatomy of a Logline

Your 25-35 word loglines should include:

- Protagonist
- Setting
- Stakes of the story
- Obstacles or source of antagonism
- Climax

For example: *'TITANIC' – An affluent young woman falls in love with a poor drifter aboard a doomed ocean liner and together they struggle to stay alive as the ship sinks into the freezing Atlantic Ocean. – (32 words)*

'Titanic' is much more than this logline. In fact, you could write that logline a dozen different ways and still express the core of the story. But that logline contains the essence of the story: *A tragic love story.*

That's how you will reduce your story. Write it, and then rewrite it. Zoom in, zoom out, expand, contract, add, subtract, until it's clear, simple, and compelling.

Here's another example from earlier, see if you remember it:

'ROCKY': A down and out, past his prime boxer gets a once in a lifetime shot to fight the world heavyweight champion for the title.

You see how the process works? You have an ace in your hands already available for creating your logline. Take a look at how you described the subject of your story back in the ideas chapter. You can use that as a foundation to begin shaping your logline.

After you finish your screenplay you'll likely revisit your logline to shape it and add spice to help market your work through queries to producers, agents, managers, and script contests.

But for now, think of the logline like a needle on your compass, pointing at the North Star to help you find your way when you're feeling lost. Spend a little time on it but don't let it bog you down. Just keep in mind that the clearer your logline — the stronger your story... and more attractive to others in the business.

1 TO 2-PAGE SYNOPSIS >>>>>

Here is your first shot at running through your whole story. Loose, quick, and colorful. Take an hour or so to write this. This creative synopsis will present a play-by-play of your story as you envision it. It's exploratory, and is mostly meant to jog your imagination now that you have a core structure worked out. It's sort of a bare-bones short story, loosely written in prose.

Let's assume 2 pages for sake of discussion. Use your plot structure as a guide; allow ½ page for Act 1, ½ page for Act 2-Part 1, ½ page for Act 2-Part 2, and ½ page for Act 3.

CAPITALIZE character names when first introduced, **highlight major plot points**, and above all be enthusiastic in the writing.

Simply write it the way you see it playing. But now that you have done a huge part of the pre-story work, this is going to be fun and on target. Trust the process!

STRUCTURE AND SCENE INVENTION >>>>>

The storytelling process progresses from broad to detailed. First nailing down your idea in general terms, then designing a plot structure that puts everything into scale with acts, sequences, and plot-points, and onward until you're eventually obsessing over single words of dialogue. (Don't worry about it... writer's obsess.)

Crafting your treatment will generate a scene list that you'll use for writing the actual screenplay. You may have chosen a few scenes already, and the major and minor plot points are already the basis of scenes...

**Think about it. If you are, let's say, creating a scene that encompasses Plot Point 1 at the end of Act 1, it should include your hero making an irreversible choice to pursue his/her want, while doing something physical to emphasize this 'stepping over the threshold'* *moment. (Like Neo in 'The Matrix' taking the red pill. Then he literally walks over a threshold into the next room.)*

If you followed 'Structure at a Glance', you've assigned mini-themes to your sequences to define them. (Like Neo training to fight in the Matrix.) Based on those themes and your plot points, you already have a lot of clues to guide you while inventing your scenes.

(See: 'PLOT STRUCTURE BASICS' at the end of this chapter for a quick primer.)

Just remember, scene choices aren't random; they're designed to illustrate your hero/protagonist's arc and transformation. Whatever part of your plot you're creating scenes for, respect the thematic queues and major plot points directing that sequence, and dream up scenes that illustrate what the protagonist must deal with at that moment in order to reach his/her #1 dramatic want.

Here's one more example: *if you're trying to figure out what scenes you need to populate the third sequence of Act 1: 'Refusal of the Call', you may design scenes that illustrate that your hero is struggling with (or refusing) his choice to take up the call to adventure because he has not yet found enough information or motivation to enter Act 2.*

The structure you created earlier is a map of your hero's journey. Use the map objectively, but trust your gut to imagine emotional and compelling scenes within that framework.

Sound daunting? It can be. It can also be fun! If you begin with a beat outline.

BEAT OUTLINE >>>>>

With logline and plot structure in hand, the initial pass at generating scenes happens with a beat outline:

A simple list of all scenes that occur in your story.

Like everything else in this process, we build things in layers. A beat outline is the simplest form of a treatment you will make. Basically just a list of quickly concepted scene ideas, in order and inline with your structure. You make a beat outline to shake your imagination loose and create something quickly so you won't be married to it and can run through a pass of it, then toss a weak scene, move one, or invent a new one that's better.

The beat outline is the start of your fully-formed treatment. Keep it loose, be creative, have fun. Seriously, if you're not having fun, your audience won't either.

Here is an example of a beat outline for ACT 1 of:

"THE MATRIX"

1. **INCITING INCIDENT:** TRINITY talks on phone about Neo. They're watching him.
2. AGENT SMITH, bad guy, shows up.
3. Cops arresting Trinity, Trinity does impossible move.
4. Trinity runs, Smith chases, she does amazing escape.
5. Trinity disappears, learns the agents have informant.
6. Meet NEO in his apartment, contacted by Morpheus.

7. **PG 12: Catalyst:** Neo at a club - meets Trinity - she warns him that he is in danger. She mentions The Matrix.
8. Neo at work, his boss scolds him for being late.
9. **PG. 17: Foreshadow end of Act 1:** Neo at his desk – contacted by Morpheus again – guided to escape the agents coming for him.
10. Neo tries to escape out the window, decides to come back – *refusal of the adventure*, he gets caught.
11. Neo in jail - meets Smith and is offered a choice – help or go to jail – gets 'bugged'.
12. Neo wakes up in bed like it was a nightmare – called on the phone by Morpheus.
13. Neo picked up by Trinity – they debug him.
14. **END OF ACT 1: Plot Point 1: PG 30:** Meet MORPHEUS 'mentor' – Neo is offered a choice to know what The Matrix is – Neo chooses to 'take the ride'. Takes pill… walks into next room.

*This interpretation of the beats taken from viewing the movie is a good illustration of how lean you can be in describing your scene beats and fleshing out the plot.

In a feature-length screenplay you'll create about 60 scenes (60 beats in your outline.) Each scene runs roughly 2 minutes/pages - some more, some less.

Here's how you start:

- Place your title and logline at the top of the page.
- List your scenes (beats) by number. *(I like to write out the beat numbers first so I can get a birdseye visual of where I'm headed.)*

- Briefly write one short sentence or fragment describing each scene. *(i.e. - Hero meets his love interest.)*
- Physically highlight or **bold** major plot points.
- CAPITALIZE character names when first introduced.

Add the major and minor plot points to the scene list first. If you have 60 scenes, roughly 15 will be for Act 1. So you know Plot Point 1 fills scene 15. Get it? You got it! Write it in. Then develop your scenes in blocks: Act 1, Act 2-Part 1, Act 2-Part 2, and Act 3.

Write your beats out in an hour or so. Quicker if you can (but it's not a race). Let the fast pace energize your imagination and have fun inventing stuff for your character's to do. What's exciting, or moving, or visual? Can you be unpredictable, but within your structure?

Think of the beats as fluid and shift things around as much as you want to in order to explore options. Move scenes until they find the right place. Add, delete, reinvent until it starts to flow.

Here's a pro tip: get in the habit of viewing movies and listing the scenes with run times. It will give you a window into how you might create for your story.

8-12 PAGE TREATMENT >>>>>

Recall the Frankenstein scene at the opening of this chapter? It described the *"odd-but-brilliant scientific machines sparking wildly as a massive electrical storm raged outside the ancient gothic castle."* That kind of simple indulgence of description is the aim of your treatment/story now.

The beat outline you just created effectively embeds your plot structure into your story by surrounding it with scenes.

Creating an 8-12 page treatment from that lean beat outline, you will expand each beat into a short, descriptive paragraph. Within those paragraphs the opportunity for you to express yourself as a storyteller is laid out before you.

In short, it's time to write your story.

Treatment Format

(See: 'TREATMENT EXAMPLE' at the end for a sample.)

1. Number your scenes. (taken from beat outline)

2. Add INT. or EXT. (interior or exterior) for each scene.

3. Approximately 50-125 words describing each scene: Explain each scene like you'd tell a friend that hasn't seen the movie: basic actions, characters in the scene, setting, important props, what the scene is about, and suggestions of character motives, meaning, and psychology.

4. Write in prose-*like* form: don't worry about sentence structure; simply capture the moment and business of the scene. Add relevant details, mood, atmosphere, and attitude. Use adjectives. Be emotional, *energize* with emotion, and tell your story to evoke emotion.

5. *Set time signature to scenes: *this is very important!*

Timing your scenes is another bridge between art and craft. At the end of each paragraph describing a scene, add the number of scripted pages you envision needing to carry out the activity you're describing. *(1 page of script = 1 minute of run time)*

Constraints demand creativity.

Ultimately you're writing your script to be filmed and it's smart to get in the practice of planning how long you think a scene will play and to hold yourself accountable to your own plan.

Discipline is a hallmark of a successful writer.

Imagining how long you think the 'business of a scene' will take is a huge help when scripting. It keeps you on track to hit your plot points and maintain your act design. Also, totaling up page count can expose holes in your plan: *you may have too few pages or too many! Then you have to add or trim scenes.*

Setting page count also helps design events within scenes to compress the moment and force conflict, or expand it to emphasize the importance of something.

TIPS FOR ENERGIZING YOUR TREATMENT >>>>>

1. **Enter the scene late and get out early.** That tried-and-true tip is aimed at compressing scenes to elevate conflict. 'Hellos' and 'Goodbyes' aren't necessary. Enter a scene as deep as you can into the action without confusing the audience. End scenes when the main objective is gained or lost, and carry the emotional signature over to the next scene.

2. **Write in present tense.** Everything in a screenplay happens NOW, never past or future (even within a flashback). This is a point of style and also grammar. Present tense words are immediate and volatile because they change whenever the next present tense action intercepts the previous action.

3. **Turn description into action.** A character never 'begins to run', he 'runs'. He never is 'about to move', he 'moves'. She never, 'starts to breath' she 'inhales'. Instead of 'the train sped up as the hero ran as fast as he could to catch it' try something like, 'The train speeds away. He races after it.'

4. **Write in a style appropriate to your story.** Use adjectives and a cadence that reflects the style, attitude, pace, etc. of how you feel the story will play. Is it punchy, or racy, or horrific, or goofy?

Get a thesaurus if you don't have one and spice things up!

5. **Character emotions and inner motives are okay.** Your treatment is for you to know your story... inside and out. Adding description of things we can't see; emotions, thoughts, intentions, motives is okay in a treatment. But don't get carried away; the same way you might use a sentence fragment to describe an action can also express hidden elements and subtext with fragments as well.

**Tips 1-4 apply to writing the screenplay too. Using them in your treatment paves the way for writing better descriptions in your screenplay later.*

Writing is rewriting, good practice now paves the way to stronger work later.

TIPS FOR INSPIRING YOUR WRITING >>>>>

Screenwriter's words are eventually turned into images and sounds. So surround yourself with things that fuel your mind - so you can fuel your story!

1. **Make playlists of music that inspires the story you're writing.** Play that music when you need to immerse your mind in the world of your story: when you write, or whenever you need to think about your story (even before a pitch meeting).

2. **Create an image collection.** You started this in your initial research. But you can develop it as much as you want. Gather images that inspire characters, settings, and moods you want to create in your story and pepper your writing space with them. After doing all the character and plot work, you probably have a more evolved vision now... add those images in!

3. **Make a movie poster.** As an extension of your image collection, make a poster or have one made that embodies your story. *It's like a logline made visual, and it's surprisingly effective to keep you on course.*

*I recommend doing all of these things from day one of your process and continue to collect, add, and subtract from your collection through all phases of your writing process.

SUMMARY >>>>>

Your Energized Treatment assembles your entire story planning, seen and unseen, into one place. Through your treatment you *tell* your story, and soon your screenplay will *express* it.

Your treatment and structure work interactively now. If you discover problems with your plot while writing your treatment, back up, adjust it, smooth it out and make it work. Nothing is set in stone; **the whole process is fluid and alive.**

Your artist side thrives during treatment writing because you fill in all the storycraft with artistic emotion. We see everything expressed openly in a treatment. But later, the art in your script will be invisible, never told, only felt through subtext, expression, and interplay of dialogue and description.

The key for the writer is to know the invisible so you can create an environment of discovery for an audience. Because when they take the journey through your story, believing they are discovering things themselves, that's what makes an audience really feel.

That's the magic of a great story.

PLOT STRUCTURE BASICS

(revisited)

Here is a clean and simple reminder of the major elements of plot structure to keep in mind as you are writing your treatment.

Act 1: Set-up

Plot points:

- Inciting Incident

- Page 12: Stimulus

- Page 17: Call to Adventure

- Page 30: Plot Point 1: end of Act 1

Themes:

- Page 1-10: introductions

- Page 11-20: expand protagonist, set up problem

- Page 21-30: refusal of the call

Act 2 – Part 1: Passive Conflict

Plot points:

- Page 45: False hope

- Page 60: Midpoint

Themes:

- Page 30-45: Reaction to new world

- Page 46-60: Begin to transform, old ways die.

Act 2 – Part 2: Dynamic Conflict

Plot points:

- Page 75: False ending

- Page 90: Plot Point 2: rock bottom, end Act 2

Themes:

- Page 60-75: Bad guys close in

- Page 76-90: Efforts thwarted

Act 3: Resolution

Plot points:

- Page 100: Climax begins

Themes:

- Page 90-100: Defeat and wallow in misery

- Page 101-110: Return from exile, new hope

TREATMENT EXAMPLE >>>>>

Below is an example of how your treatment should look per what you've been learning here. It was written from an actual story/plot outline that was later turned into a feature length screenplay.

Because of the clarity and layout of this outline, the first draft of the screenplay was completed in about 54 hours of writing over roughly 8-days. It had few objections from producers and rewrites were surface level.

What follows is only the first four scenes of that treatment. Follow this design for all of the scenes in your treatment.

"A CHRISTMAS DOG MOVIE" ©

LOGLINE: A precocious teen girl and a special holiday dog join forces to expose a criminal department store Santa before he robs her father's store and ruins Christmas.

1. INT. - Open on a crime in progress. A darkened jewelry store, gate down, clearly closed for the night. A jewelry case seems to empty out all on its' own as jewels and necklaces slide out the back. Then, we see a dwarf/little person, in silhouette walk out from behind the counter with a sack full of loot, he joins skinny female in the center of the room, one says to the other "This is gettin' too risky. We got enough to crash out at the beach in Tahiti for a year. Whatta ya think?" The back door of the store flies open, silhouetted in backlight, a big cigar smoking Santa. Behind him, a security guard is tied up. Bad guy Santa calls out in a gravel-swallowing voice for the dwarf and girl to get moving! Hear a dog barking someplace. 1-page

2. INT. - CHLOE HAWTHORNE, 13, precocious and cute, stands at the top row of the choir section in the school Christmas play. She's dressed in a crappy elf costume, and not really paying attention. Parents, teachers, and fellow students pack the auditorium. Center stage, a beautiful/popular girl belts out a horrendous version of 'Jingle Bell Rock', with ZACK, 13, handsome, tall. Chloe bores of the moment; she cranes to look out across the audience. She spots an empty seat in the parent's section. Her friend Allie asks if her dad made it. No. She keeps craning to see if he's maybe in the back, craning high up, she slips and stumbles forward knocking into the people in front of her. The rest of the choir topples over like a bunch of dominos. Everyone crashes to the ground, props careen away knocking over. A huge candy cane knocks the lead actors off the stage, Zack too. Chloe is the only one left standing in the silent auditorium, at the top step of the choir stand, with all eyes on her. 2-pages

3. INT. - Chloe sneaks out the back of the gymnasium in utter embarrassment. Allie and her mom ask if she needs a ride. Chloe says her dad is waiting for her. Allie knows better and calls her out on it. Allie shares the fact that Chloe is going to be a complete outcast after tonight. Chloe leaves on her own. (Set up some exposition about Chloe and Zack, her mom, her dad...stuff like that) 1-page

4. EXT. - Chloe walks along a street full of closed stores. The world seems kinda scary. Nighttime, cars pass. Rain. A burly security guard in a red golf cart, KLAUSE, 70's, white hair, stops her and asks if she's alone, says, "You're not a cat burglar are you?" She snaps to and says, "Seriously, I'm only 13. Do you really think I would be just walking around alone at night by myself? And no, I'm not some stupid cat burglar. My parent's are just getting the car and will be here any second." We see that she will not only lie, but that she is a sharp kid that won't let anyone get to her. Klause states the theme: "Well, that's good that you have those parents. Because you can't get make any wish come true without a little Christmas faith." Klause takes off the other way. Chloe ducks into an alley by a dumpster and sits down to cry. She sees some discarded Christmas decorations, a feeble looking tree among them with an old broken star on top. She makes a wish "Please make my dad spend more time with me. That's my Christmas wish." <u>INCITING INCIDENT ABOUT PAGE 5-6</u> 2-pages

. . .

*Notice that by Scene 4, roughly 5 minutes into the story, the Inciting Incident is called out. It landed within the first 10 pages/minutes, but also much sooner than 10 minutes which is good. *(It could be argued that the Inciting Incident even happened on page 1 of this story. In other words, it can happen as soon as the opening scene.)*

When you're done writing your treatment, revise it until it feels smooth and flows. Make notes to yourself about anything important for when you're writing the script.

Once finished, print it out, or have it ready on your computer as a reference. Trust me, the first draft of your screenplay will be much easier with a good, fully-baked, treatment in hand!

"ANY TIME YOU **GET TWO PEOPLE** IN A ROOM, **WHO DISAGREE ABOUT ANYTHING,** THE TIME OF DAY, **THERE IS A SCENE TO BE WRITTEN.**"

- AARON SORKIN

A FEW GOOD MEN
THE WEST WING
THE SOCIAL NETWORK
MONEYBALL
THE AMERICAN PRESIDENT

CHAPTER 7
POWERFUL SCENE DESIGN

WHEN IN DOUBT, START A FIGHT! Okay, not in real life, but in stories it's all about characters fighting for what they want.

It doesn't have to be a knock-down drag-out fistfight or yelling match. It could be a romantic comedy with two lovers whispering to each other in bed, each competitively trying to land the last kiss of the night, thus proving who loves who more. But it's still conflict.

Conflict is King!

Just watch Will Farrell and his onscreen family in 'TALLADEGA NIGHTS: THE BALLAD OF RICKY BOBBY' in the scene when they argue during dinner about which version of Jesus is best. Even in this ridiculous movie, and in a scene with simple staging and setting, the writers still designed conflict that is character-revealing, foreshadowed plot turns, and delivered light-hearted comedy gold.

THE SCREENWRITER'S WAY, and your growing writer's process, has filled your arsenal with tons of tools by now. All of those tools come to bear in scene design, where your characters start walking and talking (and fighting) in pursuit of their goals.

Designing powerful scenes rests heavily on you revealing enough interior information about your characters to *get the audience emotionally invested.* It will come out in the form of subtext. (*HINT: Farrell and family weren't really arguing about Jesus.)

This chapter prepares your scenes for a heavyweight emotional infusion. With some seemingly simple questions, you'll emphasize scene relevant, character-revealing parts of the information you have already created. And you'll dig deeper than you knew. Relying on your knowledge of the character's inner worlds you are about to supercharge them to fight for what they want.

By the time you complete this exercise, for all of the scenes in your treatment, you will know exactly what to write in your scenes to deliver sharp, poignant, and memorable drama.

SCENE BASICS >>>>>

- Scenes occur in one location and time.
- If you change location or time, it becomes a new scene.
- Each scene has a unique structure with objectives and stakes fought over by each character present, creating a 'rising action' of increasing intensity.
- Each time intensity levels up, that denotes a 'scene beat'.
- Each scene has a beginning, tipping point, and ending.

Design scenes to run for 2 to 3 pages:

Scenes can be any length, from an eighth of a page to as many pages as you want. However, they should be long enough to develop the moment, but short enough to condense and heighten conflict.

Enter late and exit early:

Open deep in the scene with only enough lead-in to hit the audience with information to fuel conflict. Exit the scene when someone wins and there is still enough emotional charge to pull the audience into the next scene.

Raise the stakes at each beat:

Characters will try to get what they want with the least possible expense. They should try and fail throughout the scene to get to their goal. Failure forces them to 'raise the stakes', pressing their opponent harder and increasing the conflict. Each time we witness them raise the stakes equals a **scene beat.** You will likely have 3-5 beats per scene on average. *(Again... not written in stone, but a good rule of thumb.)*

Target the tipping point:

Every scene will have a moment when, whoever is driving the scene, stands at the edge of losing their objective. The tipping point moment happens after they have consistently raised the stakes, driving it to its dramatic peak. At that peak, they launch their biggest, best argument or attack.

Carefully design your tipping point, but like all things in this process, if you discover a better solution as you write... adjust, and rewrite.

SETTING THE STAGE >>>>>

Imagine a movie set prepping to shoot a scene... Production design builds sets, actors run lines, the Director blocks movement, Cinematographer adds lights, and many other crew work; Special FX, sound, etc. Sound familiar?

That's because you already created those 'exterior' things. You've prepped for your scene work by defining genre, setting, subject, and characters. Now, all those pieces are active in your scene.

But there's more, you also need **motivations and subtext**. You've got to have emotion or the power in your scene will be missing.

Your structure, especially the sequence themes, now guides the creation of your scenes. i.e. - If you're at **Act 2, Part 1: passive conflict, sequence pages 31-45 – *Reaction***, you might need a scene where the hero struggles like a fish out of water. That 2-3 page scene might have him/her engage some antagonistic element to expose an old, reactionary way of thinking in the hero. Soon squashed, it forces the hero to move forward and find a new way.

For example: 'AVATAR': soon after Jake leaps off the waterfall (into Act 2, a threshold crossed), he is hunted by wild dogs. He reacts by lighting a torch and trying to drive them away. Typical fish out of water, human-soldier behavior... that ultimately fails him.

A scene exposes something about the characters or moves the story (plot) forward.

Once you know where a scene occurs in the story, with sequential themes guiding you, you're ready to answer some questions to shape the scene structure and prepare to add subtext.

SCENE PRIMER >>>>>

Scene Primer Questions at a Glance:

Answer each of these scene design questions for every scene you want to write (or rewrite), and you will be using one of the most powerful tools I can give you.

Let's get familiar with the Scene Primer questions, then we'll really unfold them up in the coming pages.

1. What is the CONTEXT of the scene?

Answer questions 2-5 for each character in the scene

2. What is the overarching dramatic want of the character?
3. What does the character want from THIS SCENE?
4. Will the character get it? A simple yes or no.
5. What happens if he/she doesn't get it?

6. What is the text of the scene?

7. What is the subtext of the scene?

8. What time of day or night does this scene happen?

9. Where does this scene take place?

10. What is the purpose of this scene?

11. Who drives this scene, motivates it, makes it happen?

12. What does the scene-driving character want?

    Text:
    Subtext:

13. What forces of antagonism block the scene-driving character?

14. What do the forces of antagonism or character want?

    Text:
    Subtext:

15. What is the tipping point?

16. What does this scene ask and answer about the hero?

SCENE PRIMER: SUPERCHARGED >>>>>

If you've ever watched a prizefight, you know exactly what's going on. Two ultra healthy fighters in a ring ready to pummel each other, surrounded by a stadium of cheering spectators. Exciting maybe... but it becomes compelling when you know about the fighters as humans, and the road they traveled to get to this 'fight-of-fights'. As the ringside commentators talk about the struggles and obstacles the fighters face, you learn about the insides of those competitors' lives. Those commentators are there to:

Create emotional investment.

Simple actions and settings are not emotionally charged. We need to know the interior of characters and what's at stake for them in order to get emotionally invested.

That's where the Scene Primer questions enter the picture.

LET'S GO!

1. WHAT IS THE CONTEXT OF THE SCENE?

Context: the circumstances that form the situation for an event or idea.

Answer this question by giving a brief description of what led to this scene. You might include actions, dramatic moments, and a goal that was previously attained or lost. The context might also include the thematic signature of the sequence where the scene occurs in the plot.

The goal is to get a general picture of where you came from, where you are, and what's about to happen in the present scene.

For example, this is how I would describe: 'INDIANA JONES: RAIDERS OF THE LOST ARK', the scene when Indy sees Marion for the first time: 'Indy has made a choice to seek the Ark of the

Covenant, a super-powerful artifact that would be one of the greatest archeological discoveries of all time. It's in danger of being stolen by Nazis who might be on its trail. If the Nazis get it, they could take over the world. Indy has just flown half way around the world to Asia in order to find the first and very important piece of the puzzle in finding the Ark, an ancient artifact, a headpiece to the Staff of Ra, that is being held by his former lover, Marion.'

Answer questions 2-5 for each character in the scene

2. WHAT IS THE OVERARCHING DRAMATIC WANT OF THE CHARACTER?

Dramatic want: The #1 most important desire of a character that drives and defines them throughout the story.

You should have a defined dramatic want for every lead and supporting character. The protagonist most importantly; which was defined during your idea set up and character biography.

*When answering this for each character use their name specifically or it can get confusing later when you visit your notes.

For example: 'INDIANA JONES': Dr. Jones 'Indy' wants to save the Ark of the Covenant so he can save the world, and be a great archeologist.

3. WHAT DOES THE CHARACTER WANT FROM THIS SCENE?

The dramatic want of your characters govern each of them throughout the story, but in each scene there are smaller, scene-specific wants that each character present will have.

These wants are immediate, present tense, and directly related to the context of the scene that is happening.

The scene-specific want should also aim toward attaining the over-arching dramatic want.

For example: 'INDIANA JONES': Indy goes to find Marion, whom he believes has an artifact he wants, a headpiece to a staff that he needs to unlock a critical piece of information about where the Ark of the Covenant is hidden.

Indy wants the headpiece (scene want). Indy wants to find the Ark (Dramatic want)

4. WILL THE CHARACTER GET IT?

Answer 'YES' or 'NO' as to whether your character will get his/her scene-specific goal.

*Often, the protagonist will not get what they want. Or if they do, a new problem will be introduced that draws us into the next scene.

For example: 'INDIANA JONES': NO. Indy DOESN'T get the head-piece, sort of... Marion ends up having it, but she won't give it up without her joining Indy's adventure. That adds complication and CONFLICT.

5. WHAT HAPPENS IF THE CHARACTER DOESN'T GET IT?

Describe what will happen to the character and the story if he/she doesn't get what they are after. Will bad things happen? Will the Antagonist win? Will someone die? Etc.

The consequences of this character not gaining his scene-specific goal will define how he/she fights for it. Being immediate, he/she should be fighting intensely.

For example: 'INDIANA JONES': if Indy can't get the headpiece, his journey ends. He knows Marion has it and he must get it! (His intensity is primarily illustrated when the Nazis arrive and he will fight to the death for it. And he'll fight for Marion.)

6. WHAT IS THE TEXT OF THE SCENE?

Text: subject or theme of a discussion. In scene design terms, 'text' is the obvious surface of what the characters are talking about. *('Talledega Nights': Which Jesus is best.)*

For example: 'INDIANA JONES': Indy tries to talk Marion into giving or selling him the headpiece. He describes the piece and explains how he knows she has it. The surface discussion is all about the object: the headpiece artifact.

*This can be aided by the setting and props in the scene.

7. WHAT IS THE SUBTEXT OF THE SCENE?

Subtext: underlying motivation or agenda. In scene design terms, 'subtext' is the hidden agenda, and it supplies meaning.

For example: 'INDIANA JONES': Indy and Marion have a romantic history that Marion is pissed about, because Indy left her. Now he needs her and she's going to use that to manipulate him, because she knows how important this is to him both externally and internally.

The subtext of this scene is really about the magic inside things. The magic of love and the magic in the headpiece. It's subtle, but it creates the true soul of the story. Will Indy believe in the power of the Ark? Is Indy 'true of heart'? Marion embodies this theme.

'Text' and 'Subtext' work hand-in-hand with each other. With careful exposure of subtext we reveal character, and conflict of a much deeper kind reveals itself.

8. WHAT TIME OF DAY OR NIGHT DOES THIS SCENE HAPPEN?

This question might seem too simple to even answer, but consider what happens at different times of day. If your scene is set in an inner city alley at noon, the sun will be bright and people will be around. If the same scene occurs at midnight in the same alley, it'll be dark and empty. (Dangerous things lurk in the dark.)

Knowing time of day exposes opportunities for you. It can also be a constraint that forces you to be more creative.

For example: 'INDIANA JONES': Indy finds Marion deep in the nighttime. Not many people around and her bar is closed. It could be romantic... but when the Nazis show up (like thugs in a dark alley at night), it emphasizes how there is no one around that could help Marion or witness what is about to happen.

That immediately elevates the stakes.

9. WHERE DOES THIS SCENE HAPPEN?

Like question #8, this question can open opportunities and also be a constraint to demand creativity. More than anything, questions #8 and #9 help you visualize your scene. You must invent props, the set, the environment and more. Including visualizing the staging of the actors.

And remember: your set is alive! It can be a source of antagonism or even an aid to a protagonist. It offers scene specific choices that can illustrate themes, reveal character, or create conflict in your story. **Character movement (staging), like crossing the room at a specific moment during the conflict, is a great way to announce a scene beat.**

For example: 'INDIANA JONES': Indy finds Marion in her bar, but it's deep in the mountains in Asia. The bar itself looks like a relic of a different time. It also exposes Marion's character: strong and independent (Also a sort of metaphorical 'emotional exile'). She just finished taking part in a drinking competition ('filled with spirits'. Can anyone say 'subtext coming'?), and is maybe tipsy enough to 'speak her mind'.

You can witness how 'alive' a set is when the fight breaks out with the Nazis. A red-hot fire poker is used to raise the stakes immediately. It gets whipped away *(metaphor = Indy is gonna whip these guys)* and starts a fire that threatens everyone and presses the stakes. When Indy is wrestled to the bar, the henchman sets fire to a spilled whiskey trough to hurt, and maybe kill, Indy. Even Marion gets in on the fun when a whiskey barrel gets shot and she drinks the booze pouring out. *(A girl's gotta have priorities, right? *Also a reminder of the spirit of the fight.)*

How will your set be 'alive' and provide opportunities for your characters to reveal themselves by making choices and interacting with it? *(In 'FORD VS. FERRARI', Ken and Carroll get into a scuffle with each other outside Ken's house. At one point, Carrol grabs a hard metal soup can to club his friend Ken, then he chooses to throw it aside and grabs the soft loaf of bread instead. That choice of prop reveals character, and the nature of their relationship.)*

10. WHAT IS THE PURPOSE OF THIS SCENE?

Every scene exposes something about the characters or moves the story/plot forward.

A scene could be designed to get a character to admit to one thing. It might be designed to push the protagonist to give up hope. It might be designed to show us that a monster just appeared, unbeknown to your characters.

For example: 'INDIANA JONES': It shows what lengths Indy will go to in his quest for the Ark. He'll face internal issues (lost love and sacrifice), and travel to the ends of the earth physically. It also introduces the love story with Marion and gives the audience a download of exposition about their backstory. And the subtext is going to set Indy up to believe in the magic of the thing he seeks.

This is a very complex scene! But held up by clearly defined scene beats to help us, the audience, keep up.

11. WHO DRIVES THIS SCENE, MOTIVATES IT, MAKES IT HAPPEN?

One character will be the driver of a scene more than any others. He/she enters with an agenda, a want, and the stakes he/she believes are relevant. With this, he/she will push the others in the scene to surrender what he/she wants.

Because conflict is king, the scene-driving character will continually increase the pressure until he/she wins, and throughout, the other characters will react with matching intensity to oppose him/her.

Knowing who drives a scene shapes dialogue and actions. This might depend on where the scene occurs in your story if the protagonist is the driver (as they often are).

For example: 'INDIANA JONES': Indy drives the scene because he wants the headpiece. He raises the stakes constantly until Marion ejects him with only a promise to give it to him later. But when the Nazis arrive, Indy leaps into action, another raising of the stakes, until he wins and continues his adventure.

12. WHAT DOES THE SCENE-DRIVING CHARACTER WANT?

The driver of the scene sets the agenda for that scene. He/she does this through their scene-specific want.

Text:

'Text' means the character's scene-specific want. We already answered that, so simply put that answer here.

For example: 'INDIANA JONES': Indy wants the headpiece so he can continue his adventure to find the Ark.

Subtext:

'Subtext' is about a character's hidden agenda. Why is this important to him? Is he doing this for money, duty, or humanity, etc.?

For example: 'INDIANA JONES': Indy wants to avoid an emotional entanglement about a history he has with Marion so he can keep his quest a secret. (She knows him too well.) He wants his adventure, but not the emotional charge.

This is why subtext is so important! It's the **supercharge** to your powerful scene. Marion exposes Indy's insides. *i.e. – He wants history and adventure, but without emotion (or hocus pocus, as he states earlier in the story). Marion forces emotion into the story and teases it out of Indy. Now the Ark is more than simply a thing. It has greater relevance because Indy will need to believe in its power. He has to feel.*

**No unfeeling hero ever saved the world.*

13. WHAT FORCES OF ANTAGONISM BLOCK THE DRIVING CHARACTER?

The antagonist, or the forces of antagonism, provide conflict. And conflict pushes your protagonist forward toward his/her goal. The greater the source of antagonism, the harder the protagonist will have to fight.

You can simply list them here. They can include characters, environment, setting, etc.

- Marion
- Nazi henchmen

14. WHAT DO THE FORCES OF ANTAGONISM WANT?

All characters want something, even the antagonist. The answer to this question should be a scene-specific want.

Text:

'Text' is the antagonist's scene-specific want (probably the same as, or in direct opposition to, the hero's want) so just put that answer here.

For example: 'INDIANA JONES': Marion wants to run her bar and be left alone. But after Marion agrees to give Indy the headpiece... tomorrow, a new force of antagonism enters in the form of the Nazis. They want it too, so they can take over the world.

Subtext:

'Subtext' is the hidden agenda underlying the character's want.

For example: 'INDIANA JONES': Marion wants answers about why Indy rejected her love and abandoned her. She holds the head-

piece hostage until she gets answers. Then, the Nazi henchmen want it, but what they really want is supernatural power.

15. WHAT IS THE TIPPING POINT OF THIS SCENE?

You want it? How far will you go to get it?

Characters fight for what they want. When one character pursues something and another repels their attempt to get it, one or the other will raise the stakes and try again. At the moment the stakes go up, that announces a **scene beat**. Those beats contribute to a rising action that peaks at a point of maximum pressure…

TIPPING POINT:
The critical point in a situation, process, or system beyond which a significant and often unstoppable effect or change takes place.

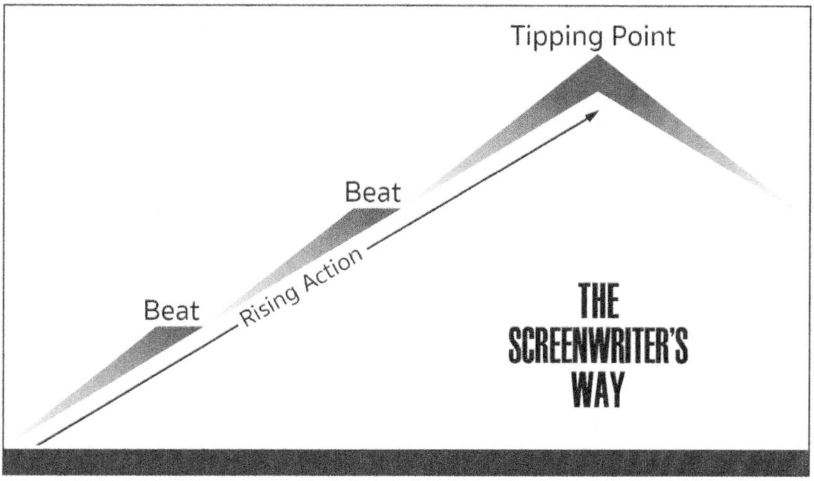

Scene Beats and Tipping Point

Beats and tipping points provide choices for characters. **And choices reveal character.** Remember your bios? How far is your character willing to go? Will he/she only try to talk you out of it, or do they resort to threats, or go all the way to violence?

For example: *'INDIANA JONES': Indy wants Marion to give him the headpiece (subtext = he wants the prize without the meaning/magic.) She wants to be left alone to drown her sorrows (subtext = she wants proof that he's changed, and won't just take the prize and run.) The scene opens with Indy arriving at Marion's bar in deep in the mountains of Nepal right after she wins a drinking game and clears the bar for the night (set and setting). In the first* ***BEAT****, he flat out states his want, 'I need one of the pieces your father collected.' To which, she responds by punching him in the jaw. END of Beat. (And OH BOY! We understand Marion immediately!)*

Throughout the second ***BEAT****, they argue (rising action), he apologizes about their past and the exchange provides exposition about their backstory and the headpiece and his mentor, her father Abner's death. This back and forth tells us he won't get it by asking, he won't get it by apologizing or 'false charm' (magic, remember the Ark?), and he can't run to an alternate source, her father, to get it. He's got to get it from Marion and he's not getting any closer to achieving his want. So then Indy raises the stakes by offering to pay her. She resists and he offers more (you gotta go all the way buddy). So she takes the money, but tells him to 'come back tomorrow, Indiana Jones'. (She's reiterating her true desire by testing if he will leave her in exile. And mocking his attempt at charm by using his full name.) So, he leaves empty-handed; he gave up his money (also establishing a little bit of trust between* *them in doing so), he doesn't have the headpiece (leaves without money or his want), nor does he get her forgiveness (his inner journey to 'hero' is in peril). End of second Beat.*

This beat also initiates the ***TIPPING POINT****. Because he only has one tool left in his arsenal… he has to fight for MARION. It's important to note that these beats and turns unfold with sharp announcements (punch in jaw, offer of money, kicked out the door). But the beats take a moment of time to mature before the next thing happens.*

During the space after the tipping point is announced, Marion resets the scene with only some brilliant acting (by Karen Allen), expressing that the money isn't what's important to her, she's a little sad… seems like she actually wanted Indy. It also tells us that Indy can't become the hero if he doesn't believe in the magic of love (and the magic of the Ark of the Covenant.)

*Unfortunately, or fortunately for Indy, the Nazis show up, thus providing the stage for him to truly show what he's willing to do, and what's truly important… Marion, because he certainly would have saved her whether he got the headpiece or not. Indy will put his life on the line to save her (that's what makes a hero)… and because he makes that choice he wins the prize (the headpiece) and more importantly, her partnership, and maybe her devotion during his adventure. *The fight sequence with the henchmen has its own series of escalations, but they don't change the dramatic beat structure because of the definition of Indy's want.*

You would plan these beats and tipping point in a Scene Primer as simple as this:

- Beat 1 = Indy simply asks
- Beat 2 = They argue and he offers to pay
- Tipping Point = Nazis show up, Indy fights to the death

This tipping point is beautifully designed. It puts Indy under maximum pressure and peril because he has to fight for his life, fight for his love interest, and for the headpiece. If he loses any of those, he's sunk. He's also now openly on the Nazi's radar, even if he wins. This scene also speeds up the story clock and raises the stakes for the entire plot.

Questions 1-14 in the Scene Primer set you up to design your scene tipping point. You have the wants, the subtext, the purpose, and the stakes by way of knowing what will happen if the scene-driver doesn't get their prize.

You can play with the shape of a scene by adjusting where you place the tipping point. A steady climb and a sharp finish might suggest that a character is willing to crush an opponent and run. A more even arc with multiple beats before and after the tipping point might suggest that the winner wants to cajole the loser, or continue to convince them to join the cause before moving on.

So, now you should take the time to design your tipping point for each scene. How will it expose your hero's character? What action will announce it? Write it down. You only need a short sentence, not an entire description.

And if, in the course of screenwriting your scene, you find the scene flat, or dull, or pointless... you now have a scene framework and a tipping point you can look back on to redesign and raise the stakes!

16. WHAT DOES THIS SCENE ANSWER ABOUT THE HERO?

By the time the scene concludes we should have learned something about the 'character' of the characters. Specifically the hero. This contributes to their overall character arc.

Did they change? How? Did they exhibit a trait we didn't know before? Like honor, or ambition, or the will to trust, or compassion. It can also be a will to fight and the ability to perform certain tasks.

For example: *'INDIANA JONES': Indy entered the scene as a matter-of-fact guy who seemed to be more or less 'on the job'. (Even seeming something like his antagonist.) In previous scenes Indy even conveyed that he didn't believe in mystic stuff and hocus-pocus. He believed in the science of archeology. But through engaging Marion and the exposure of the subtext, he showed that he had morality that went beyond the surface. In effect, he proved that he was worthy to take up the cause of this supernatural artifact that could summon the power of God.*

This scene asks, and answers, whether Indy is a virtuous man.

In addition, Marion proved to be tough as nails, utterly filled with the courage of her convictions, and worthy of the adventure herself. Marion became the moral compass of Indy's quest!

*Whatever is revealed about your hero contributes a tiny piece of their overall conviction. By story's end, when he/she arcs fully, that conviction will be on full display.

SUMMARY >>>>>

Writing is making choices, it's not guessing what will happen. The Scene Primer questions get easier to answer the more you use them. The focus you gain with them gives you power to make better creative choices throughout writing and rewriting. In addition, preparing your scene design this way leads to more powerful dialogue, and dialogue/action interaction while scripting because you know ahead of time what needs to happen dramatically.

By now you know your characters better than you know your best friend. You're thinking about setting as 'alive', and your scenes are **emotionally primed**.

Most importantly, you know your story!

You're ready to dive into scripting POWERFUL scenes!

"THERE ARE NO RULES IN FILMMAKING, ONLY SINS, AND **THE CARDINAL SIN IS DULLNESS.**"

- FRANK CAPRA

IT'S A WONDERFUL LIFE

CHAPTER 8

DYNAMIC DIALOGUE AND DESCRIPTION

SUCCESS IS IN THE DETAILS! And writing the script is most detailed part of the craft of screenwriting. It requires that you write and rewrite every sentence, every word, and every punctuation until your story sings. There is nothing extra in a script, and every single word counts. You'll hone your script, slicing out every bit of fat until it is a lean, mean work of art that grabs readers by the throat and does not let go until FADE OUT.

I can't, and won't tell you how to express your art. You have to make your own artistic choices, but I can give you a handle on some guidelines that will improve your script writing.

The rules laid out throughout The Screenwriter's Way are designed to take you by the hand at first, and over the course of doing the pre-planning work they help you create a rock-solid foundation to launch your script from.

All the rules and guidelines of craft in screenwriting should be learned, practiced, and hopefully mastered. It's when you master a tool or craft that you can use it without thought. Extending it effortlessly beyond form. Through that mastery, your art travels freely and to its fullest expression.

Master the craft, free the art.

Dynamic Dialogue and Description is presented as a series of guidelines that you can use as you see fit while scripting. Some of the guides are tight and almost expressed as rules, while others are more suggestive to simply point you in the right direction.

No matter what, each of them will help you shape your writing and make it sing a little truer.

NOW LET'S SET THE STAGE FOR WRITING YOUR SCREENPLAY...

You've come a long way, so let's prime your creative mind with a few reminders of key issues:

CHARACTER >>>>>

Each of your cast has a way of being, acting, or speaking that gives them ***character***:

Distinctive nature; quality of being individual.

Cast members become *'characters'* once we assign them a place in the story and give them their distinctive nature. They'll use that nature to fight for what they want, in effect becoming one side of your argument for the value of things in your story.

There are only two reasons anything happens in a story:

1. Expose 'character' by showing how a *Character* makes choices through dialogue or action.

2. Advance plot in order to take *Characters* to the next objective or point of conflict to expose more qualities.

Characters are always fighting for what they want, whether they use dialogue or take action. There will be no extra *stuff* in your dialogue or description.

Use every word like it was gold!

USING YOUR ENERGIZED TREATMENT >>>>>

Your treatment is a map of all your scenes and effectively sets you free from focusing too much on plot structure, allowing you instead to think more artistically as you approach your scene designs. You know where you're going, how to get there, and where you started.

Now you should have your treatment close by all the time while you write the first draft of your script. All you have to do is start threading the scenes from your treatment into your scripted pages. Turning intentions into dialogue, emotion into action, and psychology into character choices.

SCENE DESIGN >>>>>

The scene primers from 'Powerful Scene Design' can be worked out completely for all your scenes before scripting (recommended), or you can do each scene as you prepare to script it, or even redo the primer questions to focus and clarify things in rewrite.

Once you have the needs, wants, and business of the scene worked out, you'll have plenty of fuel to push conflict and get the characters walking and talking. This puts you on the verge of scripting your scenes and you should have your scene primers at hand as you write the script so you can reference them.

Your characters define your scenes by the goals they have when they enter. They want something, they want it badly, and you have to determine what they'll do to get it.

Words and actions are their ammunition, and they'll continue to ramp up both until one, or both, wins or loses.

THE GOLDEN RULE >>>>>

***The Golden Rule for all storytelling, regardless of all other rules:**

Write whatever is necessary, rules or no rules, to make your work CLEAR and INTERESTING.

***The following dialogue and description guides hold true through all drafts of your screenplay, not only the first draft. In fact, they can act as a great polishing tool for rewrites.*

DYNAMIC DIALOGUE GUIDES >>>>>

Dialogue doesn't simply talk; it can express emotion, hide meanings, and expose thoughts. It should feel alive and in the moment; each line stated like it was a character's last.

GUIDE 1: CHARACTERS USE DIALOGUE AS AMMUNITION TO FIGHT!

It can be a whisper or a scream, but characters will jockey, push, pull, fight, and manipulate through their words in order to get what they want. It's never fluff. It's never extraneous. They will be economic, pointed, and goal-oriented. And they are playing to win, whether it's a small victory or a giant windfall.

GUIDE 2: USE GENRE AND STORY-SPECIFIC LANGUAGE.

In other words, style. In many cases the genre your story resides in will come with conventions about how they speak. Sci-fi fantasies might use a lot of tech talk. Crime stories may use street slang. Your genre comes with certain demands, and provides you with an **artistic license** to express things in terms of the world your characters inhabit.

Have fun with it, because the worst sin you can commit as a writer is to be boring.

GUIDE 3: ASSUME AND ACCUSE.

A great way to infuse some conflict into a line of dialogue is to have a character assume something about the other character in the scene and then accuse them of doing it.

Then turn that around and have the accused assume and accuse the first character. They'll be fighting in no time.

GUIDE 4: TURN QUESTIONS INTO STATEMENTS.

In light of assume and accuse, if you turn a question into a statement it often becomes an assumption or accusation immediately.

For example:

CHARACTER 1
Did you shoot that guy?
CHARACER 2
What makes you think that?

Or, more dynamically:

CHARACTER 1
You shot that guy!
CHARACTER 2
You're out of your mind!

You can keep that going for the entire scene and the sparks will get worse and worse; driving conflict higher and making your dialogue immediate, present, and dynamic.

GUIDE 5: AVOID TELEGRAPHING.

You want your dialogue to be immediate. It's ammo for characters to get what they want from someone else. So, just like a boxer in the ring you don't want to give them a little hint, or telegraph, that something is coming. You just hit!

For example:

CHARACTER 1

Well, it looks like you slept with him.

Or, more dynamically:

CHARACTER 1

You slept with him!

It seems simple, but it adds edge to the words your characters are expressing. Conversely, if you want a character to ease the blow of a line he/she is about to deliver, maybe to a loved one or a boss, you may *want* to telegraph it.

GUIDE 6: AVOID SHADOWBOXING.

Shadowboxing is a term for when a fighter throws punches in mid-air as if he were fighting his own shadow on the wall. It's practice for a fight. But your characters are in a fight. Everything happens for a reason, so even if they say a line of dialogue that doesn't land the blow, it's still a set up for a hit. Because nothing is wasted.

Dive deep into your scene and get to the conflict. Extra lead in information, 'hello's' and introductions, are usually just dulling your conflict and act like shadowboxing.

GUIDE 7: EXPOSITION AS AMMUNITION.

The best way to disguise exposition is to use it as ammunition. Get your characters in conflict about something and let the exposition be launched by each character for their own gains.

Instead of stating things like facts, they use it like a hammer to pound on the other guy.

For example:

CHARACTER 1

My bail money's all gone from your last stunt. Cops find that car here and we're both in the slam.

CHARACTER 2

I was only in there because you ratted on me in the first place. You selfish, cheating, lowlife!

Now you know a lot about these characters. Jail, cheating, one got the other in trouble, they're broke, and there may be a stolen car. They did it with conflict and it provided subtext between the two of them that you could explore later.

GUIDE 8: CHARACTER VOICE.

Characters can reveal themselves through the type of words they choose to use. A great example is Kathy Bates character, Annie

Wilkes, in 'Misery'. She refuses to use profanity; instead she invents all kinds of odd, almost baby-talk words that mean the same thing. She's revealing her character in making a choice to speak like that.

By creating unique voices for characters that are distinct from other characters you make them more interesting.

In other words, don't let them all talk alike.

GUIDE 9: AVOID BEING 'ON-THE-NOSE'

'On-the-nose' is a term for dialogue that bluntly states what a character wants or what his intention is. Sometimes even stating inner desires and emotions that can't be seen. Or other times flatly stating what he's about to do or has already done.

For example:

CHARACTER 1

I think that mechanic is trying to cheat me.

Or, more dynamically and less on-the-nose:

CHARACTER 1

That hack is trying to sell me my own car in pieces.

Another example:

CHARACTER 1

If you don't go to school you'll become a failure.

Or, more dynamically and less on-the-nose:

CHARACTER 1

Successes don't stay home. And they don't deliver pizzas.

First drafts are chock full of on-the-nose dialogue. It's often a stepping-stone for us as writers when we are searching for our story. Finding and rewriting on-the-nose dialogue is also a great opportunity to add subtext, style, attitude, and voice to the rewritten dialogue.

**TIP: Purposely writing on-the-nose is a great way to break a writer's block about what a character should say. Then rewrite!*

GUIDE 10: DIALOGUE IS INTENTION.

No matter what a character says, it is only what he/she *intends* to do. (Except exposition.) By virtue of that, it's a tool of manipulation that can conceal things. It can also foreshadow things. It can reveal things inside him/her that he thinks are important and will influence him; like emotions, ideas, or thoughts.

But without action all words are intention. When your character finally makes a choice, expressed through action, you will be revealing whether his/her words had the meaning and influence he intended.

Something else to consider: with words, a character can lie. But actions are truth, because they can't be taken back.

DYNAMIC DESCRIPTION GUIDES >>>>>

Description needs as much thought and care as dialogue. It's not simply a way to describe settings and actions. It's a way to shape them into **moments** and expose character through the action!

GUIDE 11: ACTION IS TRUTH.

As stated earlier, dialogue is intention, and action is truth. This means that when your character does something it exposes his/her choice through action.

For example:

Maybe a dog is barking too much; does the character gently usher it out of the room, or throw it out the window?

Actions are real because they happen and can't be undone. They can bolster a character's statements and prove him/her to be righteous, or betray his/her lies by showing that they never intended to do what they said.

Actions also come with reactions from the character themselves, another character, or the world around them. Those actions and reactions propel plot forward.

GUIDE 12: THE 3-LINE RULE.

Keep your blocks of description to no more than 3 lines of text. (You can have more than 3 sentences. But only 3 full lines of typed text across the page.)

Your description should not require more than that to explain something, if it does then you should be leaner or the action of that moment is running on and you should break it up into a new distinct action.

GUIDE 13: LEAN, BUT INTERESTING.

This reinforces the Golden Guide of being interesting, but it bears repeating. In keeping it lean, you don't have to write in full grammatically correct sentences. Fragments are okay in screenwriting.

Within those fragments and sentences, you should keep a cadence appropriate to the genre you're writing. Make them hit, then move. Keep things moving. Use adjectives, but spare them for only what's necessary.

GUIDE 14: NO '**IS**', NO '**ARE**' AND NO '**ING**'.

To create more punch, and keep things action-oriented, don't allow yourself to use 'is' or 'are' in your description of the actions your character is involved in. That works in conjunction with dropping 'ing' from the action word.

For example:

The stolen car is speeding down the highway.

Or more dynamically:

The stolen car sped down the highway.

Another example:

The lovers are passionately making love.

Or more dynamically:

The lovers passionately make love.

It's a small change that will have a huge impact to the urgency of your description and the actions your characters take.

GUIDE 15: SHOW WHAT YOU WANT US TO KNOW.

Your descriptions should never state things that the audience can't see; thoughts, hidden emotions, intentions, backstory, and relationships. (Okay to do in a novel, not in a script meant for film.) You have to create ways to dramatize everything for the audience.

Film is a visual medium and requires that you show everything you want us to know.

For example:

Jenny fumed with anger.

Or more visually dynamic:

Jenny balls her fists and glares at her attacker.

Everything in your story has a relationship to something else that can expose the unseen. Whether it's a person that they can have dialogue with to expose information, a dog they can pet (or toss out the window) to expose their character, or an object they choose in order to express desires.

If a character is hungry, he can get a sandwich instead of stating that he's hungry (we can also hear in a film... so his stomach can grumble). The action reveals his hunger; his choice of food, and how he goes about getting it will reveal his character and be added dimension for him.

GUIDE 16: WRITE YOUR INTENDED PACE.

Your description should take as long to read as the action you're presenting. In other words, however long it takes to have a character perform the action is how long it should take to read it.

For example, a fast-paced moment:

John runs through the front door. It bangs open and he dives on the terrorist. They slam onto the wooden floor of the cabin.

Or more dynamically:

John plows through the door and slams the terrorist to the cabin floor.

Another example, a vibrant slow-paced moment:

Their eyes lock on each other as she drifts around the room. She dims lights until only their silhouettes remain.

You can expand or contract moments with your words. It's a tool to control pace and add drama, suspense, or amplify action. You're putting your reader on pace, without *telling* the pace.

GUIDE 17: USE STORY AND GENRE-SPECIFIC LANGUAGE.

Description is the place to really paint the world your characters inhabit. Imagine the genre you're writing and the kinds of adjectives that can add flavor without hurting the economy of words.

For example:

Horror genre: 'ethereal' instead of 'ghostly'

Romance genre: 'smoldering' instead of 'hot'

Action genre: 'race' instead of 'run'

These are simple changes to individual words that give them attitude, direction or passion. Every genre has words that can help tease out the tone. They can add a whole new elevated dimension to your description with just the simple use of a thesaurus.

In the words of my UCLA TFT screenwriting professor and pro comedy writer Fred Rubin:* *'Funny words are funny.'***

GUIDE 18: WRITE IN PRESENT TENSE.

Everything that happens in your screenplay happens NOW. By making things happen in the moment, it adds urgency, intensity, and immediacy.

Characters are never 'about' to do something, and they never 'start' to do anything. They either do it, or they don't do it.

For example:

Billy started to climb the tree.

Or more dynamically:

Billy climbs the tree.

Another example:

Billy ran after the ball.

Or more dynamically:

Billy chases the ball.

Present tense and immediate. You want whoever reads your screenplay to feel constantly propelled forward and hang on your every word.

GUIDE 19: MAKE DETAILS UNIQUE.

This is the world you're creating and everything in it offers you a chance to illustrate what you want. When describing objects, places, or people give them specific types of things that not only describe the object but also infuse personality.

For example:

~ A **muscle car** might be better described as a **1969 Camaro**.

~ A **revolver** might be better described as a **.44 Magnum**. ('The most powerful handgun in the world,' says Dirty Harry.)

~ A **hat** might be better described as a **fedora** or **Stetson**.

~ A **big dog** might be better described as a **Rottweiler**.

Create a vivid world so there are never any guesses about what you, the writer, intended. Every choice you make is a character's choice, or sets up a choice your character makes. Every choice exposes character. Every choice illustrates your story and defines the narrative. So make your choices specific.

*This also speaks to the production of the film. Don't leave things open to interpretation for others to figure out. Not if it's critical to your story… and it's ALL critical to your story!

GUIDE 20: FILL THE AIR.

Always give your characters something to do, even when it would appear like they are seemingly doing nothing. If you want to give a character a moment of pause, fill that moment with a story-relevant action that helps demonstrate what's happening inside that character.

For example:

Clark runs to the center of the bridge and pauses.

Or more dynamically:

Clark runs to the center of the bridge. He grips the railing and stares anxiously into the water below.

Another example:

Bruce waits nervously for Sarah to enter the room.

Or more dynamically:

Bruce sits on the edge of the bed chewing his nails until Sarah enters.

If you leave gaps in action with a 'pause' or some other way to create a slower pace or provide some 'air' to the moment, then someone else will have to fill in your gap. Whether it's the actor, director, production designer, or other crew-member, someone will have to invent something to happen in that pause or gap. Don't leave it to chance, because it's almost guaranteed that it won't be what you intended!

DIALOGUE AND DESCRIPTION INTERACTION >>>>>

Real mastery of dialogue and description happens when you get them working interactively. Each builds on the other to create full expressions of your character and their world. The interplay reveals character and exposes the unseen, the mystery we're all dying to know.

Characters also each fight in different ways, which exposes their attitude toward life. Some fight with intelligent words, some with profanity, and some with actions both harsh and subtle. The way they fight, the choices they make, the lies they tell, truths they reveal, and actions they take all expose their values, and character.

Something magic happens in the dance between the description and dialogue; subtext, motivations, and values are revealed. Juxtaposition is created. When the unseen is exposed you create drama, and can hopefully generate emotion in our audience because they can then relate. Ultimately, storytelling expresses change through character arcs, and reveals your story's conviction.

SUMMARY >>>>>

Hopefully you're seeing between the lines now too, to grasp how art and craft are intermingling to create your screenplay.

Each guide and rule of craft helps shape your artistic choices, and even create opportunities for them.

Now rewrite your dialogue and description until it sings and crackles on the page. Let it be alive!

The Guides at a Glance

THE GOLDEN RULE:
Write whatever is necessary, rules or no rules,
to make your work CLEAR and INTERESTING.

DIALOGUE:

GUIDE 1: Characters use dialogue as ammunition to fight.
GUIDE 2: Use genre and story specific language.
GUIDE 3: Assume and Accuse.
GUIDE 4: Turn questions into statements.
GUIDE 5: Avoid telegraphing.
GUIDE 6: Avoid shadowboxing.
GUIDE 7: Exposition as ammunition.
GUIDE 8: Character voice.
GUIDE 9: Avoid being 'on-the-nose'
GUIDE 10: Dialogue is intention.

DESCRIPTION:

GUIDE 11: Action is truth.

GUIDE 12: 3-line rule.

GUIDE 13: Lean but interesting.

GUIDE 14: No 'is', no 'are' and no 'ing'.

GUIDE 15: Show what you want us to know.

GUIDE 16: Write your pace.

GUIDE 17: Use story and genre specific language.

GUIDE 18: Write in present tense.

GUIDE 19: Make details unique.

GUIDE 20: Fill the air.

"I TRY TO PUSH IDEAS AWAY, AND **THE ONES THAT WILL NOT LEAVE ME ALONE,** ARE THE ONES THAT ULTIMATELY END UP HAPPENING."

- J.J. ABRAMS

REGARDING HENRY
FOREVER YOUNG
ARMAGEDDON
JOY RIDE
FELICITY
ALIAS
MISSION: IMPOSSIBLE 3
LOST
SUPER 8
FRINGE
STAR WARS: EPISODE VII

CHAPTER 9

CONVICTION AND THE FOUR 'C'S

WE BEGAN THIS PROCESS in the 'What to Write' chapter zoomed way out and examining your motivations. Then we zoomed in closer and closer until we arrived at 'Dynamic Dialogue and Description'. Now, like in so many other places in writing, we zoom out again and go back to where we started, with you and the heart of your imagination.

CHARACTER, CONFLICT, CONCLUSION, CONVICTION.

Those four words are what's known as the **Four 'C's** of storytelling. This book walked you through each of the first three. I believe I took special care in not pushing you toward artistic choices. I wanted you to have the tools, and know how they work, so that you can express yourself through the framework.

You learned **CHARACTER** by building bios, and then expanded them by taking them on a journey through your plot.

You developed **CONFLICT** through understanding Structure and then Scene Design, and especially by adding the Tipping Point.

You expressed, and probably honed, your **CONCLUSION** multiple times since first stating it in the 'Capture and Magnify Your Idea' chapter.

But did you reveal the courage of your **CONVICTIONS**?

Conviction:
The quality of showing that one is firmly
convinced of what one believes or says.

In life, you must have conviction about what you believe. That is essential to your own Hero's Journey. Without a doubt this is true for artists and writers. Maybe writers most of all. You are leaders, shamans of story, guiding people into new frontiers of thought and emotion. You are presenting a way of life and a point of view through your art. Your story, and what happened to your hero, is how you see the world and **by the end of your story, you need to express whether the outcome was worth the journey.**

This goes all the way back to Chapter 1 and your very first mini-task; answering 5 questions about your favorite movie. Question #5 asked you, *'Did the protagonist get what they wanted by the end of the movie? Was getting it (or not getting it) good or bad?'*

Most importantly it asked that last question:

Was getting it (or not getting it) good or bad?

The answer to that question is the core of your conviction.

Chapter 1 said a lot about trusting your intuition, and following your heart into what inspires you. I hope you see how key that is now. Because if you went all the way through creating a story and didn't express a conviction, then why did you write it at all?

From that first question onward, the rest of the process laid out in THE SCREENWRITER'S WAY leads you to expressing your convictions through your story. Right to this spot where I'm sharing the Four 'C's with you. So...

Do you believe that what you wrote embodied the courage of your convictions?

From a functional, writerly point of view, the simplest way to express whether what happened in the story was good or bad is via the protagonist's journey.

When the outcome arrived, and they got (or didn't get) their dramatic want, was that better for their life? Better for their world?

Did it express a core human truth that we can all learn from?

The expression of your conviction is what gives your story a point and a purpose. It's the thing people hold dear in their hearts. It transforms lives and worlds. So when people witness your hero transform and beat the odds, and they in turn feel an equal sense of courage in themselves to challenge life, only then you have successfully become a conduit of emotion, and you're an artist.

YOUR FINAL TASK:

Master the process and write a story
that makes me feel what inspires you.

I double, dog, dare you.

"GREAT **ART** COMES FROM
MASTERING THE **ARTIST.**"

- BRIAN CRAFT

THE SCREENWRITER'S WAY
REALITY'S EDGE: THE SIXTH MIND
WAY OF THE SUN

AFTERWORD: THE WRITER'S LIFE...

STORYTELLING IS CHALLENGING... *but rewarding*, and both for the same reason.

It's because while you're making choices to determine how your story world works and how characters will make choices toward their hero's journey, you're first having to ask yourself how *you* would make those choices, and then how you might do it differently in order to affect change.

Stories are more or less roadmaps for personal growth. You're examining your inner self, and that's an essential part of the writer's journey. In the process, your work becomes not only a reflection of who you are and how you see the world, but also presents an ongoing challenge to continue mastering the craft, and yourself, so you can create stories that share your insight and with greater impact.

Bottom line: writers are seekers of truth. (or need to become so.)

This task requires you to study the world around you with objective eyes. Seek out other art and stories, and study them. Find out what resonates with an audience and understand why they responded so you can use that in your own work. Study psychology and sociology and art history. Learn what makes people tick. Free yourself of bias so you can see people's character, and not only their surface.

Most of all, you should be out experiencing life as much as possible first hand. Step out on the edge and dive into life, try new things whenever you can, have weird conversations with strangers, fall in love and break your heart. Eat it all up. Examine how those experiences influence and change you. Then you can gift your newfound wisdom to the stories you write.

As stated at the outset of this book, learning how to write a great story is a lifelong process. In part from learning the mechanics of craft, and part from learning yourself. Through the course of this book you should have seen how decisions you make at one stage of story development will influence the next and even seed the ground for more choices to grow.

Now, **The Screenwriter's Way** has given you the foundation of a great writer's process. But there's more to know. There's nuance and subtlety to many of the pieces you now have. You should study storycraft like a vocation. Take the pieces and dissect them, learn different points of view and then build your own understanding of story and process.

Experiment. Take risks with your work. Break boundaries and leap into new ground. Because make no mistake, your audience is watching closely. They came to your story to learn how to make the same choices your character's make and hopefully shed a little more light on the mysteries of their own lives. They want to be heroes. You have to show them. To do that, you have know the way first. Not so that you have no fear, but so that you display the courage needed to beat any fear that arises.

We examined how creativity happens inside the box. It's because creativity requires roadblocks and limitations in order to compel fresh solutions. But as you can see, within the framework of structure and scene design and even character development and idea generation, you become the master when you build the box, too. Eventually, with continued repetition, you'll learn how to get your ego out of the way, trust your intuition at a much greater level, and let the decisions make themselves by way of the parameters you created.

Then your story and characters will come alive and surprise you. You'll write faster and decisions will happen with greater spontaneity. That's where mastery lives.

The master uses form and technique unconsciously as he/she performs, trusting that they just know. It's effortless and sublime. Like watching Bruce Lee fight, or Miles Davis play his trumpet, or a prima ballerina leap through the air as if the breeze simply took her.

Fluid, exact, and most of all free.

THE QUEST FOR GLORY >>>>>

HOLLYWOOD or AUTEUR?

On your journey to storytelling mastery, and possible immortality in art, there are very different roads to take when trying to find an audience for your work. And not all roads lead to the same arena. Knowing which road to take, or which arena they lead to, can dramatically change your writing, your experience of the game, and definitely the outcome.

Most of all, knowing where you are best suited to thrive will save you a ton of time and frustration!

Your choice of arena actually begins with knowing yourself. Same place you started when following your **intuition** to find an idea and develop it. The very same **intuition** that guided you while designing your story, and definitely the sense of self that carried you to your **conviction**.

I pulled my hair out trying to describe the Hollywood arena. But I think the immortal words of actor-extraordinaire, and my good friend, Gary Anthony Williams, best sums it up, *"You can't explain Hollywood to someone who hasn't experienced it."* And even then, it's nearly impossible to put into words.

But there's another famous line that pulls focus on it that says, *"It ain't show 'friends', it's show business."* Hollywood is in 'the business of entertainment'. It's not in the business of cultivating beautiful art and nuanced artists looking to grow and change the world. Hollywood is big money. That means films are simply 'deals' to most of the players in L.A. The town is full of producers and agents and managers (and waiters and pool guys) all trying to attach big A-list names to their project in hopes of it going from a pile of paper to Oscar glory... or box office payday. Hollywood makes spectacles. Big productions with huge special FX and movie stars for days. Stories that express lowest common denominator fair that's aimed at getting the broadest possible audience to come.

So, if you want to take a shot at the big show, then by all means you should go for it. Seriously. Don't ever let anyone tell you that you can't do something. Some of you may have a road that's longer than others to get to the mountaintop, but you can do it. I'm only suggesting that you to be aware of the arena so you don't get caught with the wrong game-plan.

I'm asked all the time if you need to be in Los Angeles to be 'discovered' or to sell a script. The answer is definitively, **'NO'**. *But...* the big game is really only happening in L.A. Every coffee shop, and gym, and dentist's office, and more than half of the lunch spots in town are brimming with 'industry-types'. And you can't sit down next to the person who could change your fortune if you're not there.

But that ain't the only mountaintop...

Do you care more about artistic meaning than the big spectacle? Are you a stanch advocate for creative freedom and are willing to fall on your creative sword to honor your conviction? Do you have the stubborn desire to experience the entire storytelling process on your own terms? Then, maybe the road of the auteur is calling you.

An auteur is the artist who writes stories and produces them for themselves. You will probably wear multiple hats, like SCREEN-WRITER... and director, producer, financier, maybe editor, probably truck driver, craft services coordinator and spooner of beans and hotdogs to hungry crew at one o'clock in the morning, and more.

You go the road of the auteur to express your art to the fullest, without interruption from other sources. It offers artistic freedom, but probably not much in the way of money. You'll have to be resourceful. You'll have to challenge your creativity in ways that may spark something totally unique in storytelling. Don't have money to make a SFX whatever? You may have to get it done with character or inference. You'll likely chase down stories and subjects that are more personal. You're a button pusher in society. You like to shake things up.

An auteur film can lead to Hollywood and the bigger fish. If it sells, Hollywood will come knocking on your door looking for more. You might be tempted to say yes. Sam Raimi made the original 'EVIL DEAD', and a hop, skip, and jump later he was doing the first 'SPI-DERMAN' and launched the modern day superhero genre. Or you could be like Jim Jarmusch (ONLY LOVERS LEFT ALIVE, DEAD MAN) and build such artistic cache that the likes of Johnny Depp and Tilda Swinton will want to work with you for no pay.

You'll take the road less traveled. You are a social visionary. You are most likely a boat-rocker. You won't find big national releases with your films and Oscar glory (most likely). But you're aims are fulfilled in the process and the work and the friends at one o'clock in the morning.

All of this is subjective of course, so take it as you will.

I'm reminded of the much-quoted words of the legendary screenwriter William Goldman (THE PRINCESS BRIDE, MARATHON MAN, BUTCH CASSIDY AND THE SUNDANCE KID), who said, *"Nobody knows anything."*

And he won the Academy Award. Twice.

There are times when even your intuition is hazy or your head filled with too many voices. If you find yourself stuck as to how to divine your path because maybe someone is offering one thing but you hoped for another, or maybe the game gets confusing and you just can't seem to put your finger on the right path. To this, I offer the words of another friend I made along my writer's journey. Two-time Emmy-nominated and SAG Award-winning actress Brenda Strong, who once told me, *"Follow the yes."*

Simple advice that can unstick you from all kinds of things. She's a smart lady, but surely follows her gut.

THE WRITER'S LIFE >>>>>

Whatever your path and goals, while you're mastering your art and opening your vulnerability to invite creativity, you need to develop a kind of dual life. On one hand the vulnerable artist, a seeker of truth who is open to change and trying new things, and on the other hand an armored guardian of that inner artist, protecting them and keeping them safe to create in a world that can seem harsh for artists.

In part, simply learning how to create a protagonist/hero is taking you on the journey to consciously understand the difference between your inner world and the outer one.

It's a dance. You will constantly be out on the fringe seeking new places. Even if that fringe is simply within your own heart. That can scare people around you, because you're inciting change. Scared people can act foolishly toward you. Like another of my mentors told me once, *'Everyone loves change, unless it's them that has to do it.'*

So while you're seeking new sources of inspiration and knowledge and an audience for your work, seek out others like you in the process. You need a tribe that understands what you're doing. You're probably a weirdo in some way. I hope so. I am. We all are in our own unique ways, whether we admit it or not. Cultivate that weirdness. Your unique voice lives there. Your tribe will understand. If they're truly your like, they'll encourage you to go even farther. They'll even provide some of that armored guardianship.

As you write and transform, your understanding of the world will expand. If you go far enough, society might even begin to seem absurd and may stop making any sense. That's probably when you're really seeing things with open eyes and on your way to a breakthrough. Keep going. Take the ride and report back what you find by way of your stories.

Be yourself, find your voice, use it to be original, and never be dull.

So, here is where I leave you. Go now and pick your path, find your personal creative North Star, and take the leap. Follow your bliss.

And above all, blaze a trail when you find there is none.

APPENDIX

THE SCREENWRITER'S WAY

STRUCTURE AT A GLANCE:

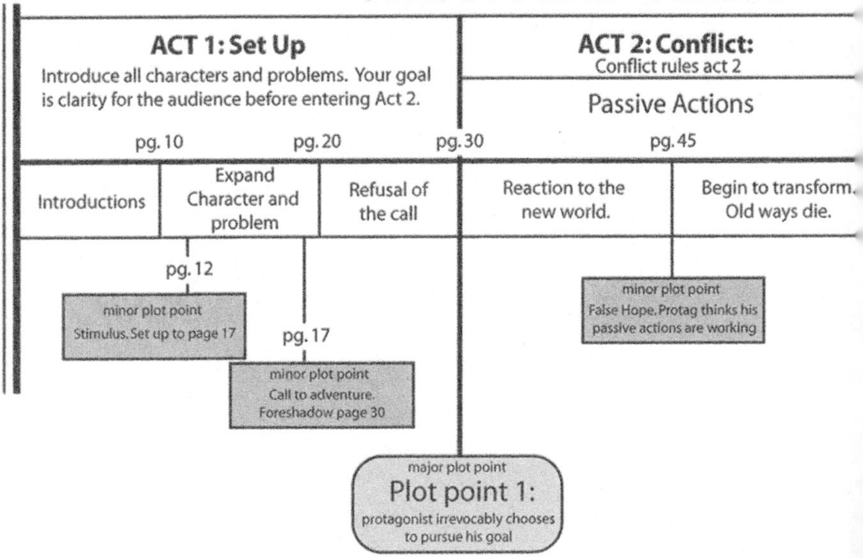

THREE ACT STRUCTURE DIAGRAM

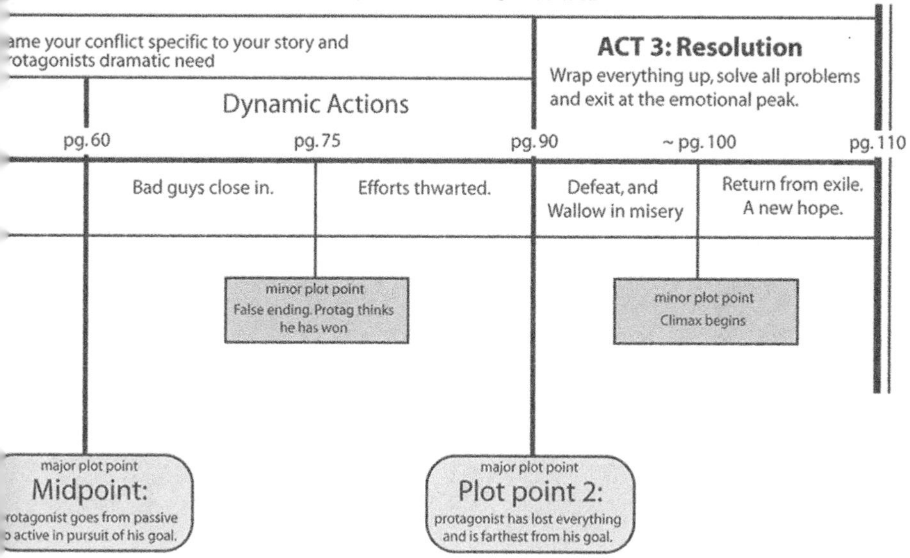

Thank you for including The Screenwriter's Way in your writer's journey. This book is close to my heart because it represents my own journey as a storyteller. The knowledge inside it was hard won. It required years of hard work, sacrifice, study, failure, and ultimately success. This book is my version of sending the elevator back down, to provide aspiring writers with great tools so that they will grow their craft, and learn to love storytelling the way I have.

So, I hope you loved this book... if you did, please consider exercising your writing skills by leaving a kind review wherever you bought it from. I enjoy reading your reviews and hearing how other writers are progressing.

In addition, your reviews make a huge difference to the success of this book. With them you can help other aspiring writers find it, and hopefully grow their love of storytelling by shedding light on the challenging task of expressing ourselves through story.

I wish you the best of luck in your writing.

Thank you, again!

ALSO BY BRIAN CRAFT

A hands on way to utilize the ideas in the book. It also includes additional exercises and guides to help you flesh out your story.

GET IT ON AMAZON.COM

WWW.AUTHORBGCRAFT.COM

ABOUT THE AUTHOR

BRIAN CRAFT

Brian Craft grew up in the Midwest, U.S.A. in something like a modern-day Huck Finn lifestyle, splitting his time between adventuring in the woods and consuming stories through endless movies and books. When the time came, he packed up his curiosity and engaged his love of movies by studying Special FX Make up at The Art Institute of Pittsburgh under the likes of Tom Savini, then continued to study Industrial Design at the renowned DAAP School at the University of Cincinnati before launching into a career creating products that sold around the world. That work swept him away to design in Paris and Seoul, and he was awarded many U.S. Design Patents. But he soon gave that all up to turn toward his burning passion for stories and began making movies, then went on to study Screenwriting under Hal Ackerman and Richard Walter at the famed UCLA School of Theater Film and Television.

Brian settled in Los Angeles where he writes screenplays and books and analyzes scripts for Hollywood. He would say he's come full-circle because now he splits his time between hiking the forests and mountains, and hanging out with other writers and artists telling tall tales. Except now, instead of only watching movies and reading books, he's creating them... *and his companions on the adventure have gotten much more interesting.*

facebook.com/authorBGCraft

instagram.com/authorbriancraft

Made in the USA
Monee, IL
01 December 2024

71907558R00125